52 Weeks of Devotions

Ben Hardister

SOTC 52

52 Weeks of Devotions from Soldiers of the Cross Motorcycle Ministry

© 2020 by Ben Hardister

All rights reserved. No part of this book may be reproduced, stored in a retrieval system, or transmitted in any form or by any means – electronic, mechanical, photocopy, recording, or otherwise – without written permission of the author, except for brief quotations in printed reviews.

All scripture quoted by the author is KJV, NKJV, NLT or paraphrased by the author from those biblical versions of scripture

Scripture quotations taken from the Holy Bible, New Living Translation, copyright ©1996, 2004, 2015 by Tyndale House Foundation. Used by permission of Tyndale House Publishers, a Division of Tyndale House Ministries, Carol Stream, Illinois 60188. All rights reserved.

Scripture taken from the New King James Version®. Copyright © 1982 by Thomas Nelson. Used by permission. All rights reserved.

Cover design by Nick Delliskave

ISBN-13: 9798572861396

CONTENTS

Preface i
#1 Stepping Up and Stepping Out 1
#2 Trouble Is Born 3
#3 Life Is A River Not A Lake 6
#4 God Has Charts 8
#5 Winnowing by the Winnower 11
#6 Sacrifice 14
#7 Pride Is Weak 16
#8 Water That's Alive 19
#9 Glad to be Dead? 23
#10 Jesus Wept 26
#11 Great and Much and Many 29
#12 Following A Formula 32
#13 Fighters Fight 37
#14 Yielding 41
#15 Sticks and Stones 45
#16 Delayed for What? 49
#17 Faulty Filter 53
#18 Four Seeds 57
#19 No Man's Land 64
#20 What's in a Name? 68
#21 What's the Problem? 73
#22 Robbed Patience 77
#23 Enthused 81
#24 Talents and Pence 85
#25 Winning and Losing 90
#26 The Chosen from The Called 94
#27 Flip Side 99
#28 The Next Morning 103
#29 Straight Lines 108
#30 One Day 114
#31 Walking Through 119

#32 Storm's Coming 123
#33 Lord of the Breaks 128
#34 Corners... 132
#35 Come a Little Further 136
#36 Roof Wreckers 140
#37 Half a Loaf 144
#38 Doors 148
#39 Bobble Head 152
#40 The Owr And Niyr 156
#41 Two Down 160
#42 3 P's 165
#43 Smorgasbord 169
#44 Green Leaves 173
#45 Port-O-Call... 177
#46 Left in Town 181
#47 Front and Back Side.. 186
#48 Shouting in the Temple 191
#49 Bay See Lay O Hee Ra Tu Ma.......................... 195
#50 Bear-Down 198
#51 Wrong Again 202
#52 Reckless Faith 206
Index of Scripture References................................... 210
Scripture by Devotional... 216
About Ben Hardister.. 219

Preface

Religion is a haven for posers who say everything and do nothing. The powers of hell welcome those who talk and never do anything. Talkers don't need spiritual guidance to accomplish a purpose because their purpose is to sit and talk and never do anything. If you are a hunting dog and not a pampered puppy you have a destiny to fulfill (Mark 16:15) and focusing on the Kingdom is the only recipe for success. *Soldiers of the Cross, 52* is a book of devotions written to help you with that recipe from men who know how to accomplish a task.

Most of the time all we need to succeed is a new perspective. The fact that you are considering reading this book of devotions says that you want more of God, and you are searching for ways to feed and strengthen your inner man and make your desires a reality. You need faith in Jesus and God who raised Him from the dead; you'll find that faith waiting for you when you start to add action to your words and go all in for Christ's sake. God wants you in the heat of the battle, for it is there that your focus on Him is not interrupted by worldly thoughts and desires. So, welcome to the heat. It's designed to keep you safe from temptations at the foot of the cross and on the right path for your life.

#1
Stepping Up and Stepping Out

The life you live for Jesus is going to be what you put into it. It takes faith to step out of the boat to be a doer of what you say or ask for. and fear will put you back in the boat every time. When you step out in faith to do something, fear is the first sign that there is a weakness in your faith. We are all subject to that weakness showing up when our attention is drawn away from the Master and onto what is threatening us.

> *But when he saw the wind boisterous, he was afraid; and beginning to sink, he cried, saying Lord, save me!* (Matthew 14:30)

In Matthew 14:29 Jesus said to Peter:

> *And He said, Come. And when Peter was come down out of the ship, he walked on the water, to go to Jesus.*

In this verse Peter was told to *come* or *erchomai* in Greek which mean *come, follow me*. Jesus must have intended to walk to Gennesaret, or He would have taken the boat with the disciples. When Jesus told Peter to *come and follow*, Peter was invited to walk to Gennesaret with Jesus, they both could have walked together for a few miles across the water to town. Peter could have gained a wealth of knowledge and tons of faith during that walk on the water. He would have had the Creator of the universe all to himself. Fear took the faith-building opportunity away from Peter and replaced it with a desperate attempt to get back in the boat. Suddenly he went from victory to defeat. The same thing is waiting for anyone who chooses to recognize fear and give it a voice.

Jesus has a miraculous walk in mind that He wants to take with you. It is a walk designed for just you and Him, and His intent is to build your faith along the way. He will allow the presence of fear to arrive so that your faith can arrive along with it. There is no faith without the presence of fear, so unfortunately it is an element of what creates faith. When fear shows up you either continue in faith or stop in fear. The proof is in the pudding and there is no walk with Jesus if you stop in fear. Choose to keep walking, as scary as it may seem. Your destiny is at stake and it is tied to the walk with Jesus. When you get to town with Jesus and step on the dry sand the only thing that will be wet is your feet as they glisten with the oil of the Holy Spirit, and you'll never be the same again.

#2
Trouble Is Born

Trouble comes as a thought or idea that you decide to act on. James says that sin is conceived. That means it has to be borne from a wandering mind; it doesn't exist on its own any more than you exist on your own without a mother and father.

> *But every man is tempted, when he is drawn away of his own lust, and enticed. Then when lust hath conceived, it bringeth forth sin: and sin, when it is finished, bringeth forth death.* (James 1:14-15)

Sin was conceived in King David when his mind was idle, and he wasn't focusing on God. He was walking around on the rooftop, probably wearing a nice robe and holding a cup of wine instead of holding the reins of a war horse riding to defeat an enemy. Trouble found David and took him down, and it will do the same thing to you when you decide to lay aside your armor and start thinking about things you shouldn't instead of engaging the enemy in battle.

> *And it came to pass, after the year was expired, at the time when kings go forth to battle, that David sent Joab, and his servants with him, and all Israel; and they destroyed the children of Ammon, and besieged Rabbah, but David tarried still at Jerusalem. And it came to pass in an eveningtide, that David arose from off his bed and walked upon the roof of the king's house: and from the roof he saw a woman washing herself; and the woman was very beautiful to look upon.* (2 Samuel 11:1-2)

Jesus Christ hardly ever changes the physical things around us to make a difference in our lives, but He changes how we look at the things around us and that changes what we do with the things around us. When Jesus Christ was teaching in the Temple and the Jewish leaders brought Him a woman who was caught committing adultery, He didn't change the circumstances surrounding her. Instead He changed how everyone viewed the circumstances she was caught up in. What Jesus said to those men about how they lived their life changed how they saw this woman from the inside and that changed what they did on the outside.

> *So when they continued asking him, he lifted up himself, and said unto them, He that is without sin among you, let him first cast a stone at her. And again he stooped down, and wrote on the ground. And they which heard it, being convicted by their own conscience, went out one by one, beginning at the eldest, even unto the last: and Jesus was left alone, and the woman standing in the midst.* (John 8:7-9)

How can we be so sure of one thing one moment and then walk away from it the next moment? How can something of great value and desire on one day suddenly become worthless on the next day? That can't happen unless the person's perspective that made the object desirable and precious somehow changes. In almost every instance the item of desire and great value itself did not change but the perspective of the desirer did. The things that matter most in life are often lost because of faulty perceptions that distort our value system, bringing the bottom layer to the top and the top layer to the bottom. The enemy of your soul is at work to change your perceptions and so is the Savior of your soul. You must choose which one to pursue. There is no neutral ground - you either fight for what is right or fight for what is wrong, but a fighter will always fight so standing on the sidelines is not an option.

If we start each day with a focus on serving Jesus Christ and a desire to follow and please Him, He will pull us toward right thinking in our minds. When we seek Jesus Christ each day our perspectives become His perspectives and we cannot be misled. His Holy Spirit fills us with His presence and changes how we perceive what is happening around us each day. We see, think, and move by the guidance of the Holy Spirit and not by human reasoning, desires or intellect. Life being lived on these terms does not happen by chance or good fortune. It doesn't occur by wishful thinking. It happens every day when you choose to make God's kingdom a priority in your life.

#3
Life Is A River Not A Lake

Life's not a lake. Many people think that life is like a lake and that the water in front of them will always be available. They think the decision to draw water from the lake on any particular day does not matter because that same water will be in the lake tomorrow. The truth is that life is like a river and the water passing by at any given moment is water you will never see again. The perspective of life being a river and not a lake will change how you see things and what you choose to take, to give, or to participate in. If what you are looking at is only coming around once, you should be serious about how you deal with it. The people and the calling in your life that are silenced, ignored, and made less important because of a faulty belief that they will always be there <u>like a lake</u> suddenly become significant. The events for the day become much more important when you realize they are passing by and will not be there tomorrow. You may think some things are the same the next day, but they are not. Other than God's love for you everything in the universe changes from day to day, whether it's a person's heart and affections or the path beneath their feet.

Successes and failures both drive a hard bargain when you decide to let them direct and steer your future. The lie that says life is like a lake allows you to walk away from the things that truly matter with the idea that you can pick them up later at the same place you left them. The things that matter most in life are invisible to the physical eye. When you travel back to the place where you left them behind your heart will tell you that they are gone, not your eyes. Pay attention to what is going on and consider the worth of what is around you. Each day there are new happenings about to begin starting with the sunrise that says the world is still here and you have this day to make a difference for God. One day this world will be gone and the things you could have done will be forever left undone. Treat today and the things in this day as a river and not a lake, and it will change how you live your life today.

> *Whereas you know not what shall be tomorrow. For what is your life? It is a vapor, that appears for a little time, and then it vanishes away.* (James 4:14)

> *I must work the works of him that sent me, while it is day; the night comes when no man can work.* (John 9:4)

#4
God Has Charts

If God charts my path before of me then I know there is nothing ahead of me that will harm me. God does not set traps, He exposes them. The reason He charts my path is because of His great love for me. He takes His time and efforts to choose the right road for me each day. If I look for Him and seek to hear His voice in the morning, I will find His path laid out before me during the day. If you follow the Lord with all your heart you will be on the right path regardless of what you may think the right path should look like.

Trust in the Lord with all your heart and lean not upon your own understanding, in all your ways acknowledge him and he shall direct your paths (Proverbs 3:5-6)

If you follow the Lord with all your heart you will be on the right path all the time. If you follow the Lord half the time you will find yourself on the wrong path half the time and instead of your days being filled with progression and victory, you will live half your days coming from behind only to lose in the end. If half my day is victorious and half my day is defeat, then my net gain is zero. If you're tired of living net zero days, then a change has to take place!

Most people want the change they are looking for right now and therein lies the rub. They want the addictive yearnings to go away *now*. They want to feel loved *now*. They want to be successful *now*. They want weight loss *now*. They want to forget *now*. This desire for a change in 4 hours is what steers us in the wrong direction in the 5th hour. We all want what we want now and it's a trap the devil laid out in the very beginning for Eve, telling her she'd know everything right now just like God.

> *Genesis 3:5 And the serpent said unto the woman, You shall not surely die: For God knows that in the day you eat thereof, then your eyes will be opened, and you shall be as gods, knowing good and evil.* (Genesis 3:5)

The devil attempted to use the same trap on Jesus, telling Him that He'd have the whole world now if He'd just bend His knee. He wouldn't have to go to the cross. It must be a very good deception, or he would not have tried it on the Son of God

> *And saith unto him, all these things will I give you, if you will fall down and worship me.* (Matthew 4:9)

Satan is still setting the same trap each day and millions of Christians fall into it when they alter the course of their commitment because things are not happening as quickly as they want.

This trap that draws people into thinking they can have what they want without waiting is age-old and probably the best trick your enemy has. Don't feel bad about falling for it over and over - but you don't have to keep falling for it. If you know the trap is there it is easier to step around it. Unplug the clock, lay down the calendar, put your eyes on Jesus, and start gaining some ground.

> *And let us not be weary in well doing: for in due season we shall reap, if we faint not.* (Galatians 6:9)

> *But they that wait upon the Lord shall renew their strength; they shall mount up with wings as eagles, they shall run and not be weary, and they shall walk and not faint.* (Isaiah 40:31)

> *The temptation in your life are no different from what others experience. And God id faithful. He will not allow the temptation to be more than you can stand. When you are tempted, he will show you a way out so that you can endure.* (1 Corinthians 10:13)

> *Those who plant in tears will harvest with shouts of joy. They weep as they go to plant their seed, but they sing as they return with the harvest.* (Psalms 126:5-6)

#5
Winnowing by the Winnower

God is a winnower. From the very beginning of your life He is winnowing you. Winnowing is flipping and tossing and letting the seed be blown in the wind until the outer chaff is separated from the seed. It is done outside in the wind, not inside where it's quiet and protected next to some cozy fireplace.

> *His winnowing fan is in His hand, and He will thoroughly clean out His threshing floor, and gather the wheat into His barn; but chaff He will burn with unquenchable fire.* (Luke 3:17)

It is no fun being flipped and tossed and knocked around when your landing is on a hard floor. That is why so many people shy away from God's winnowing fork. Rather than allowing God to remove the unwanted sin in their life by surrendering themselves to Jesus Christ, they choose to live with the dead chaff from the past that makes them useless to a lost and starving world.

Being winnowed is a process that can involve multiple flips in the air until the chaff finally let's go. The more stubborn the chaff, the higher the Winnower's fork throws the seed into the air. Why does God winnow? Because if you feed nothing but chaff to someone three times a day for weeks they will die of malnutrition. Just putting something in your mouth and chewing doesn't mean you are eating good food. The world is full of false God's and religion that offer only chaff. There has to be nourishment and life in what you eat, and God wants your life to be nourishment and life to draw a lost and dying world to Him.

> *You are the light of the world. A city that is set on a hill cannot be hidden. Neither do they light a lamp and put it under a basket, but on a lampstand, and it gives light to all who are in the house. Let your light so shine before men, that they may see your good works and glorify your father in heaven.* (Matthew 5:14-16)

If you are being flipped and tossed, don't fret. What's being pulled off and taken away from you is only the outer part of you that means nothing. You are being winnowed by a wise and loving God who has chosen you and also chosen to share the best part of you with the world. God won't let the wind blow too hard because it would blow away the seed along with the chaff. He will never let the wind blow harder or longer than what He has designed to bring the best part of you to life. Jesus selects the chosen from the called, and you are hand-picked for a purpose He has designed specifically for you.

For many are called but few are chosen (Matthew 22:14)

There is no temptation taken but such is common to man, but God is faithful, who will not let you be tempted beyond what you can take, but with the temptation will also make a way of escape, that you may be able to bear it. (1 Corinthians 10:13)

His design is not to lose you in the winnowing process but to conform you into the image of His Son, Jesus Christ. The refining of anything is a process, and it takes time and effort. The good news is that there is something worth refining in you that is valuable or God wouldn't be wasting the time to take you through the process.

And I will bring the third part through the fire, and will refine them as silver is refined, and I will try them as gold is tried: they shall call on my name, and I will hear them: I will say. It is my people: and they will say, The Lord is my God. (Zechariah 13:9)

That the trial of your faith, being much precious than gold that perishes, though it be tried with fire, might be found unto praise and honor and glory at the appearing of Christ. (1 Peter 1:7)

#6
Sacrifice

At the moment I have all I need-and more! I am generously supplied with the gifts you sent me with Epaphroditus. They are a sweet-smelling sacrifice that is acceptable and pleasing to God. (Philippians 4:18)

When we give something that is a sacrifice on our part it pleases God. When we give something that cost us nothing, not so much. Why then do so many people think that returning what doesn't belong to them qualifies as a sweet-smelling sacrifice? When Paul talks about the sweet-smelling fragrance of sacrificial giving, he is talking about a gift that someone gives that belongs to them, that they are not bound to give. It is not a sacrifice to return what isn't yours. Ten percent of what a person earns does not belong to them, so they have given nothing when tithing. They have only returned what was not theirs to begin with. Yet they fully expect an abundant blessing from God for returning what was already His. Giving back what isn't yours will keep you from being labeled a thief, and anyone who lends something to someone appreciates getting it back in good condition. The act of obedience by returning a tithe puts you in a class ahead of most Christians and you will be blessed for that obedience. But the sweet-smelling fragrance that reaches heaven and gets God's attention only comes when you start giving part of what is yours that you aren't obligated to give. King David understood this principal when he gave his hard-earned money to Araunah.

And the King said unto Arunah, Nay but I will surely buy of thee at a price; neither will I offer burnt offerings unto the Lord my God of that which costs me nothing. So David bought the threshing floor and the oxen for fifty shekels of silver. (2 Samuel 24:24)

When a part of your daily focus is to bless God with something of value, His focus will be the same coming back to you. If you and God are both lining up the future to do the same thing, who gets the better part of that deal? Take advantage of this truth and watch your life explode with blessings. Pay attention to the opportunities to give that come your way; they are designed by God to see what is in your heart.

#7
Pride Is Weak

You can be weak enough to succeed or strong enough to fail when you have a humble mindset.

Though the Lord is great, He cares for the humble, but He keeps his distance from the proud. (Psalms 138:6)

Cast me not away from your presence; and don't take your Holy Spirit from me. (Psalms 51:11)

According to the Psalms there are occasions where the God of Heaven doesn't want certain people around His throne room when they are engaging in certain activities. Many people think that they can enter into God's presence at the drop of a hat regardless of what they believe or what they are engaged in doing. Thinking that way doesn't make it true. Jesus said that following darkness as light is *really* dark. As in *no hope* dark!

But if your eye be evil, your whole body shall be full of darkness. If therefore the light that is in you be darkness, how great is that darkness! (Matthew 6:23)

Believe it or not, many people look at their pride as a good thing that separates them from the rest of us sinners, or the rest of us uneducated, or the rest of us ugly folks. There are thousands of instances where pride convinces the carrier that it is a good thing that makes them different.

Embracing pride is a sure-fire recipe for failure. Those who are unwilling to accept failure in their task or calling will attack pride wherever they find it with every ounce of their strength. If, in fact, God resists those who are proud as His Word says, then failure awaits anyone who decides to give pride a safe harbor in their life. If you really believe and trust that it is God's help that brings success to your efforts, then you will fight what stands in the way of receiving His help. When you choose to fight and resist pride, God will fight and resist those who come against you.

We can all think of prideful people who, from an outward appearance, have become very successful, but inside they are full of darkness. Light and dark cannot occupy the same space, and where there is a lack of light it is dark. The only light to a soul in the universe is Jehovah God. If that God is absent, then theirs is a dark soul, period. When you choose to embrace pride, you choose to embrace darkness.

Why would anybody want to embrace pride? Most Christians wouldn't but the worst part about pride is its ability to hide in plan site. Pride convinces the vessel that it rides in that he is there as a friend and not an enemy and the thoughts and emotions he brings are only present to preserve and protect that vessel. The strength of pride is deception. Pride works hard building walls around the things we doubt and fear to keep them from being seen by other people. We may perceive that to be a good thing, but it is a deception sent from the prince of hell who lost everything because of his pride. Make no mistake – he is trying to give you the same fate, which will alienate you from God just like him.

You are never so strong as when you realize your weakness without God, and you become willing to open your heart to Him and others. The only sure way to win the battle against pride is to do the very thing the prince of pride refused to do—to worship and honor God and to not think more highly of himself than he should.

In all you do, start by recognizing that you are nothing without God. Everything you have is a gift from Him and those gifts are meant to be used for Him to benefit others. Those who are truly grateful for what has been given to them and not what has been earned by them are usually a far distance from the house of pride. They are welcomed into God's throne room for His favor and His advice on a daily basis.

For by grace are you saved through faith; and not of yourselves: it is the gift of God. (Eph. 2:8)

#8
Water That's Alive

The Holy Spirit is referred to as Living Water in the Bible. It is the Spirit that Jesus puts in you when you accept Him as your Savior and His Holy Spirit causes an instant birth of a new life inside you.

Jesus answered and said unto her, if you knew the gift of God. And who it is that says to you, give me to drink; you would have asked of him, and he would have given you living water. (John 4:10)

And Jesus said unto them, I am the bread of life; he that comes to me shall never hunger; and he that believes on me shall never thirst again. (John 6:35)

This same Holy Spirit came upon Mary and a new life began to grow inside her. That new life was Jesus.

But while he thought on these things, behold, the angel of the Lord appeared unto him in a dream, saying, Joseph, Son of David, Fear not to take unto Mary your wife: for that which is conceived is her is of the Holy Ghost. (Matthew 1:20)

If you have accepted Jesus Christ as your Savior you now have living water flowing in you and a second life, a spiritual birth and life, to go along with your physical birth and human life.

Jesus answered, Verily, verily I say unto you, except a man be born of water and of the Spirit, he cannot enter into the kingdom of God. (John 3:5)

Before you had only been born once, so you were going to die twice, one death in the physical and one death in the spiritual. But now you have been born twice so you will only die once in the flesh, not in the spirit.

The Spirit alone gives eternal life. Human effort accomplishes nothing. And the very words I have spoken to you are spirit and life (John 6:63)

For what shall it profit a man if he gains the whole world, and loses his own soul? (Mark 8:36)

When you drill a deep agricultural water well into the aquifer below and find water for a vineyard or orchard, you have to "develop" the well after the water has been found. Without developing the well, the full production capacity or reliability of the well cannot be determined. When developing a well, the well is pumped until the level of the water falls and the well cannot continue to produce water at a given rate. When this happens, the pump man will slow the pump motor to give the well a chance to recover and replenish. When the water level rises and returns in the well it is pumped again until the supply of water fails again. This process of pumping and drawing the water down until failure can happen multiple times. The process is designed to clear the well of drilling mud and debris, and it opens up the fissures of the well allowing maximum production of water. After several of these pumping cycles, the well will settle into a certain number of gallons per minute. Once the steady number of gallons per minute is established the well is pumped at that number for several days to determine if the well will continue supplying that amount of water over time. Only then can it be considered a reliable well. The most valuable wells are those that maintain their given number of gallons per minute even during a drought.

The Living Water that was placed in you on your Spiritual birthday is only valuable to others if they can drink it too.

Neither do men light a candle, and put it under a bushel, but on a candlestick; and it gives light unto all that are in the house. (Matthew 5:15)

When this Living Water within you has little outflow, its usefulness is limited. When it fails to produce any flow of water, it is of no use at all. God wants to develop your ability to produce many gallons of Spiritual Water to refresh a lost and dying world, and the more water available in the well, the more the well has to be pumped. The Lord Jesus Christ is the spiritual Pump Expert, and He knows what your well can produce. He will work your spiritual man, drawing out of you the living water He has put in you. He knows what you are capable of and He knows what is needed to remove the debris from your heart and mind. Jesus knows what it takes to open up the deep fissures of your spiritual understanding so that His Living Water can flow through you in a sufficient amount to make a difference to a thirsty and dying world. Don't fret or run from the process of allowing more of God's Spirit to flow through you as you grow and are developed by God. When you feel like you can't go any further and you have given all you've got, He will give you time as your well is replenished with His Living Water. This is how wells are developed, physical or spiritual, and this is how God will develop your spiritual well as you go through life serving Him.

How much water will you allow God to run through your well?

For unto whoever much is given, of him shall much be required: and to men who have been given much more, of him they will ask even more. (Luke 12:48)

#9
Glad to be Dead?

Then Jesus said unto them plainly, Lazarus is dead. And I am glad for your sakes that I was not there, to the intent that you may believe; nevertheless let us go unto him. (John 11:14-15)

The word in the Greek that is used in the above verse for glad is *chairo*. This word is interpreted as: *to rejoice or be exceedingly glad*. So Jesus wasn't just 'oh well' happy. He was really happy!

In the times that Jesus walked the earth the Jews believed that a soul stays close to the grave for three days and may enter back into their body during that time. Jesus waited four days (John 11:17) before going to the house of his friends. After four days there would be no debate that it was Jesus who raised Lazarus from the dead and not just Lazarus himself who decided to step back into his body. Perhaps some might say that he was never actually dead at all. People make up all kinds of crazy excuses to explain God's miracles as something that happened by chance or unusual circumstances. Many Christians who profess faith in Christ have second thoughts in the back of their minds that the miracle that just took place in their lives was something else, something other than a miracle. How can you build and grow faith in God by the miracles that He does in your life if you don't actually see the events as miracles? Those lingering thoughts that say what you experienced was not a miracle are from Satan, and they are designed to discount the power of God working in your life. If you don't believe it was God that stepped in from the supernatural world to bend the principles of the physical world for an event that just took place, how can you believe God for the miracle that you need right now?

God knows the mind games and endless doubts that we are subjected to that rob us of the faith we need to succeed. God wants us to fight and win the battles that lie ahead of us. Jesus will arrange the need for miracles just like he did by delaying his arrival at Laz's house. All we need is faith in Him for the miracle to happen. Jesus showed up late on purpose with a purpose in mind: to build His followers faith. Will you let Him do the same for you?

It's hard to have faith in an unproven God. You can have a lot of hope, but faith comes to those who experience and see the power of a living God demonstrated before their eyes.

The above verse says that Jesus was happy. Who doesn't smile when they are happy? You may be going through a rough patch and wondering why things continue to get worse when you have cried out to God for help, and the last thing on your face is a smile. When that happens, remember this story and realize that Jesus is smiling. He is smiling because He knows what He is about to do. He's not going to do it in a way that the power of His rescue and deliverance can be minimized by the possibility that it could have happened without His intervention.

#10
Jesus Wept

The last devotion, #9, showed Jesus rejoicing or *chairo,* and in the midst of same story we see Jesus weeping

Jesus wept. (John 11:35)

Everybody should have some Bible verse memorized and John 11:35 is a good place to start. Not only is it short and easily memorized, but the message of John 11:35 packs a powerful punch to lift up your faith in Christ and pound down the doubts of the enemy.

Jesus knew what was going on with Lazarus, and that he had been dead for four days. He knew the pain Martha and Mary were experiencing because of the loss of their brother. But Jesus also knew that He was going to roll the stone away from the tomb of Lazarus and bring him back to life within the hour. If Jesus was happy to delay His arrival at the house of Martha, Mary and Lazarus the way the scripture says He was, and if Jesus purposely arranged His late arrival to benefit them and build their faith in Him, why would He start weeping when he saw them in distress and crying? Jesus would not be weeping because His friend Lazarus was dead—He knew He was about to raise Lazarus from the dead. He couldn't be sad out of compassion for Mary, Martha and their friends who were mourning the death of Lazarus, because they were all about to be astounded and rejoicing when Jesus raised Lazarus from the dead. So why did Jesus start crying when He looked at His friends in the midst of their circumstance? Why is the shortest verse and the blunt statement of *Jesus wept* inserted into the Scriptures?

If you read the events leading up to the death of Lazarus, it is evident that His death was no mistake. It was allowed by Jesus. Jesus controlled His delay in coming to the house until Lazarus was dead so He could have a triumphant entrance to the house of Mary and Martha as the Son of God. Instead of belief and triumph, He found unbelief and indignation that He showed up late.

Jesus wept because after all He had said and done to show them that He was the Son of God and Master of this life and the life to come, they still did not believe in Him. He wept because of their unbelief in who He was.

Jesus still visits the homes of His friends who are believers and finds them weeping and in turmoil because of a circumstance that He allowed to build their faith. Just like His friends of old, many of His friends today don't realize that Jesus is the Creator of the universe and nothing is too hard for Him. When Jesus shows up something that's dead can come back to life if you will recognize who He is and remember His arrival may not be late. It might be right on time.

> *Greater love has no man than this, that a man lay down his life for his friends, You are my friends, if you do whatever I command you. From now on I call you not servants; for servants don't know what their lord does: but I have called you friends; for all things that I have heard of my Father I have made known to you.* (John 15:13-15)

#11
Great and Much and Many

How great is the darkness you follow if you think the light you are following is actually darkness and not light? (Matthew 6:23)

The Greek word used in this Scripture when Jesus says darkness is <u>*posos*</u>, which means *how great, how much, how many*.

If you want problems that are great and much and many, then following your own light that is actually darkness will do it, according to Jesus.

Why would anybody purposely choose to follow darkness? There are a few twisted individuals who will seek darkness to follow, but most of us are looking for the light and we pursue it when we think we have found it. Many people equate financial success with following the light and they think their success proves that they are on the right path. They are wrong. What they possess can only be weighed by worldly wealth in dollars and cents. The false light of accomplishment, education and self-worth has seduced them into seeing their path as light instead of darkness without Christ. They have an endgame or parachute designed for their exit from their work or company. They have planned for their financial security for a few measly years on this earth but left their eternity to chance. Thinking themselves smart, they have become utter fools. (See Romans 1:22.)

This is a madness of epic proportions that someone would choose to spend all their time cleaning one spindle of the railing in front of their home and never step back to consider the condition of the whole house. The deception of darkness masquerading as light allows such foolish actions, and there is a price to be paid for rejecting such a great gift of salvation

> *So what makes us think we can escape if we ignore this great salvation that was first announced by the Lord Jesus Christ himself and then delivered to us by those who heard him speak?* (Hebrews 2:3)

> *Where your treasure is there also shall your heart be.* (Matthew 6:21)

> *You can't serve God and money* (Matthew 6:24)

There is nothing wrong with human accomplishments until we allow them to give us our sense of self-worth and define who we are. Only what is done for Christ will remain as a topic of conversation in Heaven.

Jesus sums it up nicely with a simple question:

What would it profit a man if he gains the whole world and lose his own soul? (Mark 8:36:)

And the Greek word for *profit* is <u>*opheleo*</u>: The word adds additional understanding to the meaning of the verse. It means *to be useful or advantageous*

What possible advantage does anything on earth give you when it can't be transferred to heaven?

Would a person trade places with an inmate on death row who is waiting for his appointment with the gas chamber for one billion dollars? The answer is no, because what good would a billion dollars do someone who is locked up on death row? The logic of what Jesus is saying is this: we are all on death row.

You may gain the approval or acceptance of the whole world by following a false light that lines up with world religions, mysticisms, and tolerant creeds but if it costs you your soul, what good did it do you? If the road you travel ends at the gates of hell, then what good was that road?

*Jesus said my yoke is easy and my burden is light (*Matthew 11:30)

If you follow Jesus and His light, the end of the road will be heaven and your life's work will count for something.

#12
Following A Formula

There are many ways to get a person going on the wrong path. Each of these wrong paths are designed by Satan to rob you of what God has planned for you. There is a very simple four-step formula that will keep anyone who truly seeks God on the right path and away from the destruction that waits at the end of the wrong path.

The first part of the formula starts with **acknowledging that God put His Son Jesus Christ in the highest position possible** in the entire creation and universe from the very beginning. He is the King of Kings and the Lord of Lords.

The second part of the formula is **understanding that God does not change His mind.**

God is not a man that He should lie, neither the son of man that He should repent: hath He said, and shall He not do it? Or hath He spoken, and shall He not make it good? (Numbers 23:19)

The third part of the formula is to **look at what you are following and to see if the religion or philosophy being taught lowers or diminishes the position of Christ.** If God gave Jesus the supreme position of power and authority from the beginning, anything that diminishes or replaces that position cannot be from God. God didn't appoint Jesus as the only path to Himself for just a little while until some man could come up with a better plan. Any teaching from man or religion that makes Jesus less important than what God made Him to be is following the wrong path.

The fourth and final part of the formula is to **apply the first three parts of the formula** without excuses and choose to walk away from the wrong path that you are on. This fourth part of the formula is the hardest part, but it will be easier walking away now than trying to explain why you didn't walk away later when it's too late.

Some religions including humanism are up front and bold as they denounce Jesus Christ as being anything other than a good person. That claim erases all of His power and authority right up front. However, there are others that are much more deceptive and underhanded. They claim to follow Jesus as they quietly strip Him of His power and authority.

The following are a few examples of deceptive teachings and how they are revealed by the first parts of the formula:

Praying to someone other than God/Christ:

If I can pray to someone else in heaven or earth for help or advice other than Jesus Christ, then the position of Jesus is shared and someone other than God is just as powerful as He is. This makes Jesus less important because someone else can do the same things He can.

Doing good deeds to qualify for eternal life:

This teaching says that I can earn my way to heaven by my own efforts and therefore become part of an exclusive group of good people who have earned the right to be in heaven. This makes Christ less important because my efforts have to be joined to His efforts on the cross for me to get to Heaven. Jesus needs my help to save me and His power is therefore diminished.

Being a good person:

This says that I don't need Jesus because I'm not really bad enough to need a savior or to be redeemed. If this is true, then the office Jesus holds of Savior and Redeemer is actually abolished and completely null and void without any power or authority.

Changing Jesus as the only begotten Son of God:

Mary had more sons, but God only had one – Jesus. If Jesus had brothers, then He is not the *Only begotten Son of God* and so God's sacrifice of sending His *only* Son to Earth is lessened. This claim also paints God as a liar by saying He had only one Son. Mary had more sons, but God only had one – Jesus

God was a man before He became God:

If God was a man, then Jesus would be begotten by a man and a man from a man is less powerful with less authority than a God from a God.

Teaching that there is no hell.

Taking away the existence of hell also minimizes the importance of being rescued from hell and the glory that is due to the Rescuer. If there is no hell to be delivered from, then there is no need for a Deliverer. The importance of Jesus is lessened and again it paints God out to be a liar. Jesus actually mentions hell in the Bible more than He does heaven, so He is shown to be a liar on multiple occasions which also lowers his reputation and importance as a God of Truth.

There are thousands of examples of how Satan, through men, attempts to lower the deity and power of Jesus Christ and those mentioned above are only a few. The power of Jesus is not affected by these attempts. Jesus defeated Satan forever when he said in John 19:30, *It is finished*, but His saving power and grace are affected in you when you chose to believe something outside His Word. There is no place in the entire Bible where the power of the Messiah and Savior of the world, Jesus Christ, is lessened or diminished throughout all eternity! You have to go outside the Bible for that to occur. When you leave the pages of the Bible for further teaching or amended instructions from any other book or man claiming to speak for God, you will find yourself on the wrong path.

If Jesus Christ is the Lord of your life and the pathway you have chosen to follow is God's unchanging Word, don't fall for the lie that says there are other ways to God and other books or revelations that reveal who God is. Jesus Christ has a plan for your life. Apply the formula if you're unsure of the road you are on and let His plan unfold each day in your life. Don't accept anything that says His power and authority are less than what they are.

#13
Fighters Fight

If you were born a fighter there will always be a war of one kind or another to fight. You will either fight for a cause that advances the kingdom of God or fight for something else that benefits only you and the kingdom of Satan. You may not believe that refusing to fight for God makes you a warrior for Satan, but the meaning of scripture is clear when Jesus says:

He that is not with me is against me (Matthew 12:30)

To follow God's plan for your life is a fight, plain and simple. There will always be opportunities to take the path of least resistance and relax rather than fight but giving in doesn't mean you are out of the fight. It just means that you're now fighting against what you use to be fighting for.

David was a fighter and he fought for the cause of God and the support of his brothers. One day when there was a battle to be fought David stayed home. In his mind he wasn't betraying his brothers or abandoning God and joining the ranks of Satan's army. David thought he deserved a break, or he wouldn't have taken one. He didn't see the harm in relaxing at home or he would have stayed on the battlefield. David spent 20 years living in caves and avoiding traps, so he would not have foolishly walked into one if he'd known it was there.

If King David was tripped up by taking a break, don't be foolish enough to think that taking a break from the battle won't trip you up too.

David thought he was off the battlefield and out of the fight, but fighters will always fight. Very soon after taking off his armor he found himself within the space of a few hours fighting for the cause of Satan, which was to destroy God's plan for his life and cause innocent people to suffer. The part of this story that is the most disturbing is how Satan turned David's love and loyalty to his brother-in-arms, Uriah the Hittite, into betrayal and murder. Uriah wasn't just some guy with a beautiful wife; he had spent years in the caves loyal to David and fighting by his side. Uriah was listed as one of David's inner circle and Mighty Men, thirty-seven in all.

> *These be the names of the mighty men whom David had: ... Uriah the Hittite; 37 in all.* (2 Samuel 23:8, 39)

Uriah was more than just an acquaintance and some guy in the army. Uriah was probably one of the most honorable men David knew, evidenced by the fact that he wouldn't sleep with his wife when the king told him he could, and his wife was no barker.

In 2 Samuel 11:11, Uriah replied, "The Ark and the armies of Israel and Judah are living in tents and Joab and my master's men are camping in the open fields. How could I go home to wine and dine and sleep with my wife? I swear that I would never do such a thing."

His fellow soldiers were still on the battlefield. The worst thing a man can do is to betray his brothers, and you can do the same thing when you step away from the battle and think you are no longer fighting.

You have been given a vision and calling. You have a destiny. You have been anointed just like David by the Holy Spirit to further the Kingdom of God. You have been given the strength, *(Greater is He that is in you than he that is in the world* -1 John 4:4*)* and the will to fight to further the Kingdom of God and bring glory and honor to His Son Jesus Christ. You will not be sidetracked, tricked or fooled into thinking there is no trap waiting for you. The strong man and trickster has been bound.

No man can enter into a strongman's house and spoil his goods, except he will first bind the strongman, and then spoil his house. (Mark 3:27)

No weapon formed against you will work to bring you down. (Isiah 54:17)

Keep walking the battle line and engaging the enemy to rescue those who are lost. There is no sitting the battle out and resting while someone else takes your place. There is no other you. You were chosen and the strength you need is in locking eyes with the Captain of your soul every morning before you head out the door for another day of what you were born to do—fight!

#14
Yielding

Part of the Lord's Prayer is *lead us not into temptation*, or do not let us yield to temptation.

The Lord Jesus was tempted in every way that we are tempted, yet He did not yield to the temptation. He did not sin.

> *For we have not a high priest which cannot be touched with the feelings of our infirmities; but was in all points tempted lake as we are, yet without sin* (Hebrews 4:15)

Yielding to sin can be doing something we know we shouldn't, or not doing something that we know we should. In many cases both of those things are taking place at the same time within the same sin. Jesus knew that doing what the devil told Him to do would be sin, so it was something He didn't do. At the same time He knew that He had to use the Word to win the battle of yielding. The Bible says if we know what we should do and don't do it, it is sin,

> *Therefore to him that knows to do good, and does it not, to him it is sin* (James 4:17)

Jesus was led by the Holy Spirit to that desert and He was led to use the word to defeat the temptations of Satan. If Jesus chose to not follow the Spirit and not use the Word to fight against Satan, that would have been sin for not doing what He was led to do.

We fight many times the yielding to sin on one leg and we fall over in our attempt because it's not a balanced and fair fight. A fair and balanced battle is *doing the one thing, and not doing the other*. This is a two-pronged attack, and it is balanced on both legs, which gives you a better chance of winning.

Consider this example. A man is having an affair with a woman at work. He knows it's wrong and he decides to fight the temptation, repent, and get back on track. He is led by the Holy Spirit concerning what to do and what not to do. He is shown that his thought life is what leads him to her desk, and he is given a strategy by the Holy Spirit to quit this sin and get free.

He is shown **What To Do**:

1) Capture each thought he has of her and toss it out of his mind immediately before it takes root.

2) Get up early and make more time for reading the Word each day before work.

3) Find a weekly Bible Study and participate.
4) Join a men's group for accountability.

Then he is shown **What Not To Do:**

1) Do not have lunch with her, drive to work with her or to be in a room alone with her.

2) Do not meet after work for any reason.

3) Do not explain yourself or try to justify your actions or have sympathy for yourself or her.

4) Do not dwell on the past; look forward to the future.

If someone chooses to fight the battle with only what he shouldn't do and discards what he should do, or visa-versa, then he will go down in flames as "the last of the one-legged fighters."

We are all subject to failing in our attempts to keep from yielding to sin. We need the help of the Holy Spirit and His power. Instruction from the Holy Spirit and being led by the Holy Spirit can come from many different places. He is in and part of everything around you, including the air you breath. He can direct you in prayer, His Word, a Christian brother, or a stranger at a gas station. Once you know in your heart that He has met you and shown you what to do, then pray to God and follow both sides of His instructions. Praying to Jehovah God is not a worthless tradition or useless mantra with nothing but superstitious hopes of help that may or may not come. Prayer to God is heard by

Him and powerful to the tearing down of strongholds or the sin that has been holding us back.

> *We are human, but we don't wage war as humans do. We use God's mighty weapons, not worldly weapons, to knock down the strongholds of human reasoning and to destroy false arguments* (2 Corinthians 10:3-4)

#15
Sticks and Stones

The shepherd boy David shows up to the war camp of the Israelis, but they are doing anything but war. One guy has held off the attack of one million soldiers by his taunts and their fear. It's funny, but the threat of doing something, if believed by the one who is being threatened, is actually better than doing something. Doing something means you have to exert an effort and actually spend time and energy to do what you say. But a threat, if believed and accepted as truth, has the same effect without actually having to do anything at all.

Whether or not Goliath actually had the ability to defeat any man in the Israeli camp or not didn't matter. His threat paralyzed the entire army without him having to do anything. The victory that God had planned for His people was stalled for nothing more than a threat of what might happen to them. That's all it took.

Many times, we find ourselves frozen at the prospect of moving forward because of nothing more than a threat of what might happen if we step through the open door before us.

The door was open for any soldier in the army to trust God and walk through it, but what Goliath said and how big he looked was enough to keep every soldier from believing what Jehovah God said. It rendered the whole army powerless.

If you decide to unstrap your arms and walk past the threat that has kept you standing still and paralyzed, it would be useful to examine exactly how David did it, and then follow his example.

Faith does not exist in a vacuum without the presence of fear or consequence. The presence of a threat or consequence only exists to validate the need for faith in God to challenge the threat. God had a way for David to face and defeat the threat, and He has a way for you to extinguish the threat before you too. God's way will require faith in action, and not just talk. If you want to start moving again, you must act in faith.

David explained to King Saul that he had killed the lion and the bear when they came to take his sheep and that he'd do the same to Goliath.

I go after it with a club and take the lamb from its mouth and club it to death. (1 Samuel 17:35)

If you notice, David doesn't say anything to King Saul about killing a bear or a lion with a slingshot. As a matter of fact, there is nowhere in the scriptures that says David ever used a slingshot to kill anything before the day he killed Goliath with one. David's plan was to take the trusted club he had used before, the weapon he had experience with, and fight Goliath with it. We know from the scriptures that David approached Goliath on the battlefield with his club,

> *Am I a dog that you come at me with a stick?* (1 Samuel 17:43)

David had moved in faith to confront the threat and defeat the enemy with his experienced club, but he had also been obedient to the voice of God. David had picked up five smooth stones from the brook on the way to meet Goliath. I believe using the slingshot was the furthest thing from David's mind because he went out with his trusty club. David had explained to Saul how he had killed the lion and bear and had plainly stated that he would use the same method to defeat Goliath.

> *David persisted. I have been taking care of my father's sheep and goats, he said. When a lion or bear comes to steal a lamb from the flock I go after it with a club and rescue the lamb from its mouth. If the animal turns on me, I catch it by the jaw and club it to death. I have done this to both lions and bears, and I'll do it to this pagan Philistine, too for he has defied the armies of the Living God.* (1 Samuel 17: 34-36)

The scriptures tell us that David ran at Goliath.

> *As Goliath moved closer to attack, David quickly ran out to meet him. Reaching into his shepherd's bag and taking out a stone, he hurled it with his sling and it hit the Philistine in the forehead. The stone sank in, and Goliath stumbled and fell face down to the ground. Then David ran over*

and pulled Goliaths sword from its sheath. David used it to kill him and cut off his head. When the Philistines saw that their champion was dead, they turned and ran. (1 Samuel 17:48-49, 51)

You can't hold a club and a sling and reach into a shepherd's bag unless you have three hands. David had to drop his club in order to load and fire a sling. It became evident to David as he got closer to Goliath, that unlike a lion or bear, this enemy could kill him from a hundred feet. He would never get a chance to use his trusty club on this enemy, as he planned. In the heat of the battle, he realized his plan wasn't going to work. That's when he dropped the club.

God had given him the provision for victory, but he didn't see it until the moment of confrontation. If he'd known God's plan, he would have dropped the stick when he picked up the stones.

When you're confronted by a challenge and decide to do something about it, you are no different than David. God has not changed one degree from who He was 3,000 years ago in the valley of Elah, so you know where He stands. Trust God's sovereign ability to defeat any enemy or threat that stands in the way of His plan for your life and move forward in faith. Remember that God may know a better way to defeat this enemy than you. Do remember what He has done in the past, and let those memories build your faith. But be prepared and willing for Him to reveal a new strategy to defeat the enemy, as the battle heats up and you go from *sticks to stones!*

#16
Delayed for What?

But of that day and hour no one knows, not even the angels in Heaven, nor the Son, but only the Father. (Mark 13:32)

Has the day of His return or the *rapture* been set? Or is He letting the date float? If God has delayed the date for the arrival of His Son, then what is that delay for?

We can leave the answers to theologians who like to argue about those things. One truth is very clear: God's wants more people safe with Him in heaven, not less.

Peter thought the reason God wasn't green-lighting Jesus and letting the horses out of the barn was due to God's desire for more people to be saved from destruction.

The Lord isn't really being slow about his promise, as some people think. No, he is being patience for your sake. He does not want anyone to be destroyed, but wants everyone to repent. (2 Peter 3:9)

Unless you want to say that the Bible is wrong and Peter didn't know what he was talking about, the plain and simple truth is that any delay in His coming is due to His desire for more people to be saved. What isn't so simple is why Christians think the delay is designed so they can gather more belongings, or to travel to more places to stare at more stuff?

If you are doing all you can to reach the lost, then God has you in mind as He allows time to keep rolling on. The rest of the planet is just along for the ride.

Many people, including some Christians, struggle to save more money, to buy more things, to vacation in various places so they can marvel at the creation rather than the Creator. Its prophetic and certainly is nothing that a follower of Christ should be wrapped up in.

who exchanged the truth of God for the lie, and worshipped and served the creation rather than the Creator, who is blessed forever, Amen. (Romans 1:25)

Many Christians are included in this vast wandering horde who can't wait to see the next wonder of the world. The Bible they read says these special places that they are so enthralled with are all going to burn. They have no idea why God has given the earth and mankind more time. They don't see reaching the lost as a priority and they don't plan on joining God's efforts to reach them anytime soon. They save their money to travel and stare at temporary things that offer no eternal reward, and yet they neglect what is eternal and the very reason the planet still exists - to save the lost.

If the desire of your heart is to reach the lost, then you are in step with God's desire. That is the only reason the trumpet hasn't sounded yet. If your prayer is to do more to bring in the lost, that prayer will be answered.

> *And this is the confidence that we have in him, that if we ask anything according to his will, he hears us.* (1 John 5:14)

Not every Christian is a missionary, but every Christian should support one and be engaged in the battle for the souls of men. If you are doing all you can and you want to do more, you're going to need more power.

If 500 horsepower takes you through the quarter mile at 120 miles per hour, then it will take 800 horsepower to get you through at a buck fifty. The same principle applies to the call on your life. The power and anointing that has brought you this far must increase. If you've been given more time to reach more people, you also will be given more power to accomplish the task.

Missionaries have to press to do more, and those who earn the dollars to give to the missionaries have to do more as well. Many churches and para-church organizations have starved-out the missionaries. They strive to build their own ever-expanding ministries within their own walls but neglect any work other than their own.

The people who earn the money decide where their money goes. If an organization thinks they can ignore the mission field, then you should ignore their multiple pleas for more of your money. Why would a church present the gospel in a town where fifty other churches are doing the same thing? There are towns where the gospel is not being preached. Why are those towns being neglected? If that is the mission of your church, then you should find another church.

The Giver and the Missionary are inextricably connected. Financial blessings and increase go to the one who gives to the missionary. Then the message of the work of the missionary increases as they reach more people with the Good News!

> *Yes, you will be enriched in every way so that you can always be generous. And when we take our gifts to those who need them, they will thank God. So, two good things will result from this ministry of giving, the needs of the believers in Jerusalem will be met, and they will joyfully express they're thanks to God.* (2 Corinthians 9:11-12)

Both parties to this last-day push of God, are giving what isn't theirs to others. They both give so that others can hear the truth and live. Both are going to have to give more to get more.

Jesus said:

> *So pray to the Lord who is charge of the harvest; ask him to send more workers into his fields.* (Matthew 9:38)

The Lord of the harvest wants more, which means He is willing to give more to get it. When you make giving more to God a priority in your life, God will make giving more to you a priority too!

#17
Faulty Filter

Paul was told by Jesus that he was headed to Rome and that he should be of good cheer, or encouraged, by the fact that this was Paul's destination and destiny.

That night the Lord appeared to Paul and said, be encouraged Paul, just as you have been a witness to me here in Jerusalem, you must preach the Good News in Rome as well. (Acts 23:11)

Most of us who love and worship Jesus want desperately to be on the right track while following Jesus. We pray and fast and read the Word for direction, and we trust that the path we are on is the one our Lord and Savior has designed for us. Our destiny is in the hands of Jesus and we have confidence that He is leading us, day by day, to our destiny.

If the Bible is our template for how we should roll in our pursuit to follow His directions, then the examples and the lives of others that are written in His Word are there for us to follow. We should pay attention to the details of those lives to see if what we expect to happen and what we are experiencing is similar to those who have gone before us.

If we look at what happened in the very next verse immediately after Paul heard from Jesus, we see that what took place did not seem like something to be glad about or encouraged by.

> *And when it was day, certain of the Jews banded together, and bound themselves under a curse, saying that they would neither eat or drink until they had killed Paul.* (Acts 23:12)

If Paul were looking at his circumstances from the wrong perspective, or through a faulty filter, the evil plans by a group of fanatics to kill him wasn't something to be glad about. A faulty filter lets a person look at the circumstances and believe they have done something wrong, or heard something wrong, and disaster is on the way. This perspective robs you of faith and allows fear to take hold where faith should be growing. You become paralyzed and the faith that was growing is now dying, and you can't figure out what went wrong as you slowly abandon your plans.

Jesus told Paul to be glad that he was going to Rome for a couple of reasons.

1. He was chosen for a task that Jesus wanted him to do.

> *For many are called but few are chosen.* (Matthew 22:14)

The chosen are selected from the called. When Samuel visited Jesse to choose and anoint a new king

(1 Samuel 16,) all of his sons were called to the house but only one was chosen. To be chosen for a work that Jesus needs done is a super privilege. Any born-again believer should be excited and honored and encouraged God's eyes are on them.

2. It was the Creator of the universe, who only needed to speak the Word for the sun to show up, Who told Paul he was going to Rome. If Jesus said Paul was going to Rome and that was his mission, then he knew that no matter what happened he would be in Rome.

The only thing that could sidetrack his mission would be time. As long as there were no time limits, God had plenty of room to move and perfect His will in Paul's life. If you notice, Jesus didn't say *when* He would get to Rome.

Many time's you'll miss the will of God by affixing a date to the Word he speaks to you heart. It is natural to want what God promises sooner rather than later, but it can be a recipe for being knocked out of the race.

If Satan schemes to stop the plan of God in your life you should rejoice for a couple reasons.

1. If Satan wants to stop the mission you have been given, it must be pretty important. Who doesn't like winning a fight, especially when it's against a superior opponent and there is a lot on the line?

2. When the mission is complete and the miracles it took to complete the task are behind you, your faith will have a chance to grow. This will enable you to believe for greater works and to win bigger battles in the future.

Many Christians have lots of hope, but they have very little faith because they worship an unproven God. When you arrive at the back side of a battle with a few scars, and you sit in amazement at the road you just traveled with Jesus, the hope within your heart turns to faith. You worship a proven God in your life and not just stories you've heard.

#18
Four Seeds

The story of the sower and the seed in Luke 8:5-15, Matthew 13:3-23 is thought by many to be a parable about salvation. Salvation is a part of hearing from God and accepting His Son as your savior and is certainly illustrated in Jesus's story. But the parable of the sower and the seed that goes into different kinds of soil speaks about so much more than only about salvation. It speaks to everything in your life that God calls you to do.

The King James Bible refers to the seed in the story as the *word*, and the NLT refers to the seed as the *message*. The word that is used in the parable for *seed* in the Greek is *logos*. The definition of *logos* in part means: *A word, uttered by a living voice, embodies a conception or idea, the sayings of God.*

If the story was meant to be only about salvation, Jesus would have said the seed represented the message of salvation and not any Word spoken by God, or *logos*.

Jesus said the seed represented the *logos* of God, which can be heard from many different sources as vast as God Himself. *Logos* from God can be given in a vision or dream, when reading the Bible, listening to a brother or sister, hearing His voice in prayer, witnessing something in nature, or watching a movie or TV. *Logos* from God can show up in the time and place and manner in which God determines. And when He speaks, He will never say or do anything that contradicts what is written in the bible.

God's Word or *logos* to your calling is the seed. You will always have the choice to accept or reject that word depending on the condition of your heart, or as Jesus paraphrased it, the soil where the seed lands. This is true of accepting Jesus as your Savior or talking to someone in the grocery line.

When you see and understand that the seed is any Word spoken from God, then you also begin to understand that this parable of the four seeds is tied to everything God speaks to you, or His *logos* to you.

Jesus likens God's Word to you as a seed that is plucked away, dies, has no benefit, or produces great amounts of fruit. There is more of everything when you accept and follow God's Word to you.

When a person hears a Word or *logos* from God, what they do with that Word or *logos* determines how far they get from the first to the fourth seed. The first and the fourth seed are the same seed, but either the first seed continues the progression to the fourth seed, or it doesn't.

This is the progression of the seed or the *logos* from God into the different soil of your heart:

1st Seed: Falls on the pathway and is snatched by birds.

You receive a message or *logos* from God, and it is immediately discarded as something you will not consider or do. As soon as you think of following what you hear from God, you begin to contemplate the consequences or possible difficulties and problems. Those might include embarrassment or financial hardships if you follow His Word, or other consequences. You say, "No way!" God sowed a seed or *logos* in you and Satan immediately snatched it away when you refused to follow what He said to do.

2nd Seed: Falls on shallow soil, no roots, fails in the hot sun.

You get a Word or *logos* from God and you accept that it is from God. You joyfully step out in faith to accomplish what He has given you to do. You abandon any doubt or fear of consequences and move with the faith and conviction of a disciple to follow His Word to you. The birds of the air, or doubt, couldn't snatch this seed away.

Once you start moving forward all hell breaks loose, and you start to think that you were better off before starting this crazy journey. You decide to quit and turn back to what you were doing before, when you didn't have so many problems. You doubt that God ever gave you a Word or direction to do what you're doing, and you quit and go back to the life you had before. You never make it past the 2nd seed.

3rd Seed: Falls on good soil, grows a good tree, but bears no fruit.

The Word or *logos* is received from God, and Satan was not able to dissuade you from following God. At all costs and at every turn you have stayed loyal to what you believe God told you to do. In time because you have obediently followed God's Word the blessings start to flow in your life because the blessings can't be stopped when you follow God's Word. Soon the windows of heaven start to open and there is more of everything that you lacked before

At this point Satan lets you know how important and smart you are, and most of your time is taken up buying nice things and planning a life that doesn't include making God a priority in your life or searching for the lost. You are now able to worship God at your leisure with no pressing issues. Being desperate for God's presence and direction is a thing of the past.

The third seed is the downfall of many. Once people get to the third seed, they no longer need anyone, including God. The cares of this life and the riches thereof are Satan's most powerful weapons. He saves them up for his last-ditch effort to stop you before you reach the fourth seed. Very few people get past the first two seeds and even fewer go beyond the third seed to the fourth, but there is a guaranteed way to make it to the fourth seed that is explained at the end of this devotion.

4th Seed: Falls on good soil, grows a tree that produces 30, 60 and hundred-fold.

The Word or *logos* from God is received with joy. The Word of God, or the seed, has survived and made its way to the fertile soil of the fourth seed. You have kept your focus on what God has said to you, and your main goal is to continue keeping His Word and furthering the kingdom of God. Each person is born with a throne that sits in the center of their heart and they occupy that throne with their orders and edicts according to their desires until they abdicate that throne to someone else. Furthering the kingdom of God is when the efforts of your life results in people surrendering to Jesus and asking him to sit on the throne of their heart.

The fourth seed life is full of abundance as you continue to seek God with all your heart in the midst of the abundance. Those who reach the fourth seed are very rare individuals and their numbers continue to dwindle as Christians are taught that those who follow Christ won't experience hardship. This shallow teaching is appealing to many, but it leads people to quit at the second seed when they should be pressing forward.

An illustration of the four seeds and the call of God on your life can look like this:

1st Seed. God tells you to move to Oregon. You say, "No way. I don't know anybody in Oregon and I hate the rain." So, you don't go. The birds just snatched the seed and hearing the Word is as far you get.

2nd Seed. You go to Oregon and then you get fired from your job and your wife leaves you and you say, "I've had it with Oregon, I'm going back home. "The second seed is as far as you get.

3rd. Seed. After your wife leaves and you get fired, you hang in there and keep trusting God. You start a business and become very successful. Then you say, "I don't have time for the Church or ministry. I've got too much work to do. And I've got to look at a new boat." And the third seed is as far as you get.

4th Seed. You have been blessed and you say, "I've got to find more ways to give to God. I love Him for all He has done for me." And you go on to produce fruit, 30, 60 and hundredfold.

Now that you know the progression of how Satan intends to keep you from following God's Word or *logos,* and your calling, you can prepare for the battle and recognize the attacks when they come.

Everything you do of any significance for God will be challenged by the four seeds. You must protect that first seed when God speaks His *logos* to you. Do not be afraid to consider what God is saying to you, and don't let the satanic bird steal your future without at least throwing a couple of rocks at him. The other seeds will not matter if the first seed is snatched away. Your destiny is at stake. The field of your life will grow only brown grass instead of a green tree if the seed God cast your way is destroyed before it gets a chance to grow.

Instructions for passing the Third Seed and becoming a fourth seed follower of Christ

It is very difficult to prepare and to defend yourself against the plans that Satan has to take you down during the third seed, that's because the person you will have to fight for your call and ministry to survive the third seed is yourself. When the day of the third seed comes you will want what you want. It will be the day when your views will change with your success and then your actions will change to go along with your new views and convictions. Your standards of what is acceptable are lowered to allow you to again access to sins that were not previously available to you. This will be a world of success that you have never experienced or seen before, and you can't know what it's like and how to prepare for it or how to survive it.

There is only one way to get through the third seed, but the good news is, the way through this third seed is guaranteed. It is not a hit and miss or maybe formula, it is guaranteed and here it is:

> Don't do anything while in the third seed blessings from God that you wouldn't do while in the second seed trials and testing of God.

The reason so many people fall during the third seed is their refusal to follow this simple to hear but not so simple to do instruction. Let this instruction be applied to every area of your life and follow it and you will find yourself a fourth seed follower of Christ.

#19
No Man's Land

Is there a place you can go where Jesus cannot help you? The Bible says there is.

> *Stand fast therefore in the liberty by which Christ has made us free, and do not be entangled again with a yard of bondage. You have become estranged from Christ, you who attempt to be justified by law; you have fallen from grace.* (Galatians 5:1, 5:4)

If you want to be in a spiritual No Man's Land put your trust in what you can do and not what Jesus did do. The whole idea of people finding their own way stems from the desire to be in control. At a base level, the desire for control is laced with pride and it cannot be said enough that God resists the proud. If you're walking with pride, welcome to No Man's Land where you can insist on doing things your way.

These Galatians were Christians, but they wanted to sprinkle some of what they wanted to do into the mix. Not everyone who is in No Man's Land is trying to change the basic fundamentals of the Christian religion like the Galatians, but the need for control puts them into the same boat as the Galatians. And where is that boat? It's somewhere that God can't help you.

The best way to recognize a Christian in No Man's Land is someone who is easily offended. They will only go so far with any given group and then something or someone will offend them. Once they choose to focus on the offense they are no longer concerned about where God placed them or what they were supposed to do. Suddenly in their minds, God must have changed His mind about where He wants them. And now God has a new, more righteous plan for them apart from these people who didn't appreciate them. Off they go to the next church, Bible study or ministry group. Like the foolish Galatians they follow a way of life that puts them in bondage and steals their destiny because they won't stay where Jesus put them.

Most everyone agrees with the foregoing as being true. Unfortunately, the same people who agree and say they will not get offended are among the first to get offended and leave the place were God put them. It's easy to say you won't get offended—until you get offended. People willfully take a drive to No Man's Land when they add or take away from what Jesus said to do.

When we think more of ourselves than we should, that is the beginning of the road to No Man's Land. It may take a few months or a few years to reach the destination but make no mistake - you are on your way. When we allow our sense of entitlement to take precedence over where God has sent us or what God has told us to do, then God is no longer part of the equation. The worst part of this hell ride is that most people on this road will bend what they believe is the will of God to match their actions of abandoning God's directions. Because of their bent message system and understanding of God's will for their life, most people in No Man's Land don't even know they are there. They confuse being busy for God with being in God's will, so they are always looking to replace what they left with something else *God told them to do.*

The Galatians who listened to Paul were the ones who were teachable. They did not allow what they wanted and what they *thought* was right to be preeminent over what God wanted and what He said *was* right. They did not get offended, and they stayed where God put them doing what God told them to do. Jesus could speak to them in the place of their obedience and the life they lived for Christ counted for something. The other Galatians, the ones who were offended by what they heard, went on their own way with their own ideas and never accomplished anything of any value. If you are where God hasn't sent you, your efforts are in vain.

Pride will tell the reader of this devotion *#19, No Man's Land* that the reason they left or quit what God gave them to do had nothing to do with being offended. Pride will tell them their situation is different, but it is not. Letting your emotions erase what God has told you to do is **never** the right road. Ask for clear vision from the Holy Spirit and realize that not taking offense isn't so easy when someone says or does something offensive to you. It takes the power of the Holy Spirit to hang in and get through the times of offense that come in your life. The good news is that Jesus said God would give the Holy Spirit to anyone who asks for Him

> *If you are evil, know how to give good gifts to your children; how much more shall your heavenly Father give the Holy Spirit to them that ask?* (Luke 11:13)

#20
What's in a Name?

The name Jude and Judas are Hebrew names that mean the same thing: *He shall be praised.* The Hebrew pronunciation is EE-YOU-DAS.

Jude was the half-brother of Jesus who wrote one of the books in the New Testament, and Judas was one of 12 disciples chosen by Jesus. The name they were each given at birth proclaimed *He shall be praised* but the life they chose to live decided whether or not there would be praise coming to God or heartache. Salvation and honor would come to one, and destruction, death and shame would come to the other. They both had the same name and their life was laid out before each of them, yet to be lived, and waiting for the decisions they would make from day to day that would mold them into what they would ultimately become.

Judas was all set for his name to be everything it claimed to be. He had everything that anyone would need to succeed in a life that would bring praise to

God. Judas had talent and abilities, or he would not have been able to keep track of the accounting. Out of the whole world he was chosen and elevated to be one of the 12 disciples. He was on the right path, everyday being led by God Himself. God gave Judas everything he needed for the name of Judas to be a description of his life. But Judas decided he had a plan that would add to God's plan and make it better.

When all the disciples gathered together for dinner for the last supper, Judas was given the place of honor next to Jesus. Jesus showed him that He loved him and told him that He knew who His betrayer was. Judas could have fessed up to the betrayal and been forgiven. Jesus could have still been betrayed because of the steps Judas had already taken, and the scriptures could have been fulfilled that Jesus would be betrayed by a friend - and Judas could have still been saved. Judas's name, *He shall be praised* could have been the results from the life of Judas.

Jesus knew what Judas had become so He gave him a job where he could do the least amount of damage. He put Judas in charge of the least important thing in His ministry: the money bag.

> *This he said, not that he cared for the poor; but because he was a thief, and had the bag, and bare what was put in it.* (John 12:6)

Jesus knew that His Father owned the cattle on a thousand hills, (*For every beast of the forest is mine, and the cattle on a thousand hills Psalms* 50:10) and that the money needed for their expenses would be supplied by God. Anything Judas could do to harm their finances would be the least damaging thing he could do, and the easiest to fix.

What did Judas want? Perhaps he wanted Jesus to bow-up and take on the priests and the Roman government right there. If that happened, Judas could be the new Secretary of the Treasury of the new government. Or perhaps he just wanted the money from the priests. It doesn't matter. When he decided to go off on his own, that was the beginning of the end for Judas.

Jesus showed Judas His love and mercy on the last night they were together by washing his feet and sitting with him at the table to eat. Jesus included Judas in all that He was doing for all the disciples. He never pointed a finger at Judas in front of the other disciples, not until the end of dinner when he refused to repent. During dinner Jesus revealed that He knew what was going on and thereby gave Judas time to think about what he was doing and change his mind.

Satan was enticing Judas to go off on his own with his own plan, but he had not entered him yet. When Judas refused to change his mind and decided to go all in with his plan, Satan entered him and the chances for Judas to live a life that his name described became zero.

The Bible says that Judas got up from the table and bolted out into the night, leaving the dinner and his Master and his brothers. The Word doesn't say that Judas was angry, but you can guess that he was by the fact that he left immediately without saying good-bye or, "Thanks, man, for the dinner."

> *Having received the piece of bread, he then went out immediately. And it was night.* (John 13:30)

Lots of people are doing the same thing today, and they don't even know it. They may still be going to heaven, unlike Judas, but their life is being completely derailed because they want to add to God's plan with their own ideas about what or how Jesus should do things. In almost every instance the person who refuses to change their plans gets mad and leaves, and they always find it is night when they go. It will be dark without revelations or relationship when you step out of God's will,

If you are called to be a steward, or a servant, of God, don't let the description of that title be forfeited by putting a plan in place that is different than God's plan for your life.

If you have stepped over the line and started down a different path than the one God has designed for you, stop. Jesus has a place at the table for you, where He will talk to you and restore you and get you back on track. If you'll listen and stop following what you thought was a good idea, and follow His plan for your life, everything will be all right. You may have to go through some bad times because of the events you set in motion, but you and your destiny and your calling won't have to be destroyed.

Jesus will take the negative and make it work for the positive if we follow His plan and stop following ours.

And we know that all things work together for the good to them that love God and to them that are called according to his purpose. (Romans 8:28)

Trust God's plan and get back on the road he put you on. Turn back while you still can and let the name you have been given describe who you are and not who you could have been.

#21
What's the Problem?

The stories in the Bible are a record of what God has done, and the prophesies are a record of what He is yet to do. All of God's promises to you are prophesies, because the days that lie ahead for you are yet unlived.

The lives that have already been lived by others in the Bible are recorded for you to read so that you can see what God was willing to do to help and rescue those who trusted Him. When you read how He rescued others, it helps you to believe that He will rescue you.

There are many Bible stories, and they are all designed to build your faith for the road that lies ahead as you live your life each day.

So then faith comes by hearing, and hearing by the Word of God (Romans 10:17)

Some of the stories are examples that you should follow, and others are warnings of what not to do. Regardless of their purpose, they are all written to build your faith.

There are multiple messages that God can bring to you from just one story to encourage you. That is why we should never say, *Oh I've read that story in the Bible before,* and then close your mind and spirit to what God may be wanting to say to you. The very thing you need to hear may be hiding in the scripture you think you know everything about, and the Holy Spirit wants to reveal it to you.

A common theme in many stories is the onset of trouble as soon as a person is given instructions or direction from God. We learn from reading that the trouble is usually designed or allowed by God to serve His purpose.

One example of many in the Bible is the story of the disciples who were sent across the Sea of Galilee (Mark 6:45) There are probably whole books written on just this one story, with multiple interpretations and revelations, but consider just two.

1) The Disciples did not quit.

There were 12 guys rowing all night against the wind and they were getting nowhere but they didn't quit. It would have been super easy to say, "God controls the wind, so He must be against us going across. We need to turn around." Or they could have said, "We must have heard Jesus wrong. He must have said **not** to go across the lake," and then turned back and gone with the wind back to shore. The Bible says that they were halfway across or in the middle of the Sea of Galilee or the Lake of Gennesaret.

Late at night, the disciples were in their boat in the middle of the lake, and Jesus was alone on land. (Mark 6:47)

2) The water was the problem.

The water is what could take their life. They did not have an option to turn their backs on the water and rest or think about what they were doing. They couldn't just pull over to the side of the road and think about it like in a car.

Like many other stories, trouble shows up when you're halfway into doing something. That is why the Bible is specific to say they were in the middle, or halfway across. It was Jesus Who allowed them to get halfway across before He showed up. They had been rowing hard all night and He could have shown up earlier if He'd wanted to. The threat of the rough water was the problem they couldn't escape without his help. Jesus wanted them to know that they would never reach their destination without His help with the water.

Jesus is watching you row, and He knows when to step in. When your destination becomes unsure because of the water, or whatever else is threatening your progress, He will show up and eliminate the problem.

It was the water that was threatening them, there was nothing else that could harm them without the water. It was the water that would drown them if the boat went down. When Jesus showed up, He put the water under His feet and walked on it. He showed His power over the water and took away its ability to intimidate and destroy.

So, what is the problem? Whatever thing in heaven or earth that is threatening you today, continue rowing.

Jesus will show up at the right time and show you that the threat has no power to stop you when He puts that threat under His feet.

#22
Robbed Patience

For you have need of patience, that, after you have done the will of God, you might receive the promise. (Hebrews 10:36)

What exactly does that mean? What image comes to mind when you think of needing patience? If you have the wrong image in your mind and the wrong idea of what patience is, then it will be impossible to obtain and possess it because you will reject it and find ways to avoid it.

Many people will turn the page and go on to another subject when they see the word *patience*. In the minds of many, patience is associated with endurance and pain that can be physical, emotional, or spiritual—and sometimes all three. Why would anyone voluntarily put themselves in a position to participate in learning patience?

When you understand that your success and your destiny is tied to your ability to be patient, you become willing to seek a way to make patience a part of who you are. You become willing to engage in an uncomfortable battle within yourself and the world around you when there is something to be gained.

Patience is not obtained by sitting with your hands folded and waiting for patience to descend upon you in a cloud. The word in the Greek for patience is *hypomone*, (hu-pom-o-nay) which is interpreted as *steadfastness, constancy, endurance*. Patience is acquired through effort and the greater the patience that is needed, the greater the effort that is required.

If you know that the absence of patience will cause you to lose the thing that you desire or have worked for, then you will pursue patience with all your strength and not just a casual effort. Many of us try to be patient because we know that's what we're supposed to do in certain circumstances. But we don't understand that patience is a critical ingredient in God's formula to bless us. If we knew that the lack of patience would guarantee failure, we would make sure to put patience on the top of our list and pay close attention to where and when it's needed.

If it is patience that is required for us to obtain the promises of God after we have done his will, then it is patience that the devil will try to rob you of. Your enemy does not want you to obtain any promise from God. The promises of God are manifold and many. His thoughts toward you and the blessings He has planned for you are too numerous to list in one devotion, but a good place to start is:

> *For I know the plans I have for you, says the Lord, they are plans for good and not for disaster, to give you a future and a hope* (Jeremiah 29:11)

If I know that I need patience to obtain the promise of God and I know the devil wants to rob me of patience, how do I keep from being robbed? The answer is easier said than done, but the good news is that there is an answer. There is a way to keep from being robbed.

If I refuse to accept anything less than what God promised me, then the end result will be my receiving what God has promised. Patience is the gap between the *promise* and the *possessing*. If I lock the door and don't allow anything in that was not promised to me, then I cannot be robbed of my patience.

Your enemy knows you are holding onto God's promise and trusting in His Word. He also knows when you are getting tired of hoping and waiting. We all would like to see the arrival of the promise and the end of patience sooner rather than later, so we are constantly looking for the light at the end of the tunnel. The enemy will take advantage of your situation and circumstance if you let him. He will propose an alternate plan that will bring an early end to your waiting and thereby eliminate the need for being patience and trusting God. He will create a false light that will look good to you. He will suggest a different answer or alternate plan. If you accept this alternate plan that is something less than what God has promised, then your patience has been robbed along with your faith.

When you get close to obtaining the promises of God you will be presented with a worsening dilemma, and the offer of a promise or deliverance through something that is less than what God said He'd give you becomes a temptation to accept.

The thing you can accept that will stop the waiting and put an end to the horror ride of patience may be close to what you were promised by God, but it will not be the same size or quality. It will be lacking key ingredients of what He promised. At this point it becomes impossible to stay patient and in faith without God's help, but if you ask for His strength and pray for His will, He will help you. God will give you a measure of faith to keep you from being robbed of your patience and destiny. If you possess faith, you will possess patience, one goes with the other.

If King Saul had waited another hour, he'd still be king.

> *Saul waited there seven days for Samuel, as Samuel had instructed him earlier, but Samuel still didn't come. Saul realized that his troops were rapidly slipping away. So he demanded, Bring me the burnt offering and the peace offering! And Saul sacrificed the burnt offering himself. Just as Saul was finishing with the burnt offering, Samuel arrived, Saul went out to meet and welcome him, but Samuel said, What is this you have done? Saul replied, I saw my men scattering from me, and you didn't arrive when you said you would, and the Philistines are at Micmash ready for battle. So I said, The Philistines are ready to march against us at Gilgal, and I haven't even asked for the Lord's help! So I felt compelled to offer the burnt offering myself before you came. How foolish! Samuel exclaimed. You have not kept the command the Lord your God gave you. Had you kept His command the Lord would have established your kingdom over Israel forever. But now your kingdom must end...*
> (1 Samuel 13:8-14)

#23
Enthused

It is really hard to fake enthusiasm. The best indicator of what people believe in is their enthusiasm. There are posers who pretend they believe in something, but their biggest betrayal is the look on their face when faced with an obstacle, and their actions in life don't mirror what they say with their mouth. Many people will say they trust in God but two minutes with their check book register will show you what they really believe. And when mounting debt snarls at them they fold because they know they have no faith for deliverance from a God they cheat every Sunday.

There are many places in the Bible where God shows us that He tries the hearts of men to see what's inside. Some people need to be told that they are lacking in their commitment to their beliefs and what they said they would do. Often, they don't even know they are doing it. Other people have no intention of honoring their commitments. They give lip service to gain some advantage in life, love, or financing.

There is no hope for changing the minds of those who say they believe in something when they don't. What they actually believe is hidden and not part of any conversation so there is no opportunity for them to discuss and learn and change. There is also no opportunity for you to see their lies. If you are drawn in by their words while paying no attention to their actions you will suffer harm.

If we know that God compares our actions to our words, we can bypass a lot of problem by doing the comparison ourselves. If our words don't match our actions, we can make an adjustment from our side of the table instead of waiting for God to make the adjustment from His side.

The last prophetic action of Elisha was to tell King Jehoash to strike the ground with a handful of arrows to signify victory over the Arameans.

> *Then Elisha said, Now pick up the other arrows and strike them against the ground, So the king picked them up and struck the ground three times. But the man of God was angry with him. You should have struck the ground five or six times! He exclaimed. Then you would have beaten Aram until it was entirely destroyed. Now you will be victorious only three times.* (2 Kings 13:18-19)

It was left up to Jehoash to decide how to strike the ground with the arrows. Just like other posers, Jehoash's true feelings and beliefs came out for all to see when he struck the ground without enthusiasm three times instead of five or six. The prophet was not looking for the number of times as a formula. Elisha and

God were watching Jehoash to see the condition of his heart. If he really trusted God and wanted to follow His commands he would have been jacked up and slammed those arrows in faith and anticipation of what God was going to do in his life and kingdom

Many people are taught that quoting a scripture as a formula will deliver the desired results. One, two, three and *poof!* in a lackadaisical repeating of the mantra, and what they need will magically appear regardless of how they live. God looks past our words to the condition of our hearts and the actions of our hands.

If you were in a fight and you were getting more punches than you were giving, you would be noticeably excited and enthused when the heavyweight champion of the world stepped into the room to help you. God is paying attention to your response when He steps into the room; don't let anyone fool you into thinking that He isn't. Get excited about your deliverance! Step up and make a proclamation of God's goodness and thank and Praise Him for coming to help you. Then make sure your actions and your life reflect your belief that God is in the ring with you.

At the base of all enthusiasm is faith in a God that you know will show up and make a difference. How can you have faith or be enthused about an unproven God that you're unsure of because you have never trusted Him to show up? How can you be enthused about God helping you when you know the way you're living has left Him out of your life?

If you are just going through the motions and doing what someone tells you to do, reading what they tell you to read, and saying what they tell you to say without faith and enthusiasm, you'll end up like Jehoash. There will be a few victories, but the end will always be defeat because you have no faith of your own. You'll just being doing what someone else tells you to do, hoping that things will work out.

Faith and enthusiasm are by-products of a relationship with Jesus Christ. If they are lacking in your life, ask the Holy Spirit to open your eyes to God's presence in the midst of the battle. Like Elisha's servant, you will see that there are more for you than there are against you, and that there is no reason to be afraid. Enthusiasm for God's presence will follow.

> *And he answered, Fear not: for they that be with us are more than they that be against us. And Elisha prayed, and said, Lord, I pray thee, open his eyes, that he may see. And the Lord opened his eyes of the young man; and behold, the mountain was full of horses and chariots of fire about Elisha.* (2 Kings 6:16-17)

There is Someone far greater than Elisha standing next to you. Be encouraged and enthused about what God is going to do in your life.

#24
Talents and Pence

Jesus said in Matthew 18:22 that we are to forgive seven times seventy, but it wasn't meant to be a formula that says after forgiving someone 490 times you didn't have to forgive them anymore.

Forgiveness to someone for a wrong they have inflicted upon you is supposed to be a natural reflex that comes from a grateful heart.

Jesus goes on to give an example of what a grateful heart should look like. He uses the value of money to illustrate His point. In Matthew 18:22-34 Jesus compares heaven and hell to money because everyone can imagine how great it would be to get a boatload of money for free. Money is not evil; what is done with money can be evil, but money has no life and no soul.

To fully understand the parable of forgiveness it is helpful to understand the monetary amounts used in the parable for context. A talent is 200 lbs. of precious metal or gold. 10,000 talents are equal to two million

(2,000,000) pounds. At today's price of $1,667 per ounce for gold, the total value of 10,000 talents of gold is: fifty-three billion three hundred forty-four million dollars ($53,344,000,000.)

A pence was a coin whose worth was considered to be equal to that of a single day's wage for a Roman soldier. This is not an insignificant amount of money. To pay a professional for one hundred days of labor is maybe forty or fifty grand, which is a lot of money unless you compare it to fifty billion dollars. It is important to acknowledge that in order to understand the parable. When you are wronged it is a significant occurrence not just a penny or a mite. Sometimes it is hard if not impossible to forgive until you weigh what's been done to you versus what's been done for you. When you consider the imbalance, only the worst of hypocrites would refuse to give forgiveness, and that is the point of the story. How could you not forgive a debt of a few thousand from someone when you've just been forgiven a debt of billions?

The key word in the question of forgiveness is *just*. In time we forget what we were forgiven for and lose the spirit of gratefulness. Pride of self begins to take over as we forget what was done for us.

Many people who sell a house for a profit of several thousand more than the asking price will include a few personal items, like a washer and dryer, if they are asked by the buyer. They have been given more money than they expected, and they are happy and grateful for the sale. The value of the washer and dryer is easy to give up when compared to the windfall of profit received. It is a different story when house sells for thousands below what the seller wanted and then the buyer asks to throw in the washer and dryer. The seller is paying attention to every dime from the sale and they are reluctant to give the buyer anything extra.

The reason so many people are hard pressed and reluctant to forgive someone is that they do not equate their salvation as something of great value that was given to them over and above what they had coming. When what you have been given is not an abundance you are stingy with what you have.

Jesus used the illustration of 54 billion to 50 thousand in His Word so that we would never forget how far God went to save us and how small our effort by comparison is to forgive others. When we understand that we put God in a position that required the life of His Son for our forgiveness, there should be nothing that stands in the way of us doing our part by forgiving others

The parable of talents and a pence shows it was a billion times harder for God to do what He did for our forgiveness than what we have to do to forgive others. It can be argued that the number is so high that it is meant to be a metaphor. What God did is so much harder than anything we have to do that it is impossible to calculate. If you want to bring the concept closer to home just ask yourself how much more difficult it would be to send your child away to be tortured and killed versus going next door to apologize to your neighbor? About a billion times easier to go next door is what comes to mind

Many people get to the point where they think that salvation is something they earned and deserved and there is nothing gracious about how they obtained salvation. Therefore, there doesn't need to be anything they should offer to anyone else as a gracious gift. They are like the brother of the prodigal son who never forgave his brother and offered him nothing but a cold shoulder when he returned. The brother earned what was his and he wasn't going to offer anything to anyone else, including his own brother. He didn't like that they were spending his inheritance or money on the sinful brother.

> *And he was angry, and would not go in; therefore, came his father out, and intreated him. And he answering said to his father, these many years do I serve you, I did not transgress at any time your commandment; and yet you never gave me a goat for a feast with my friends.* (Luke 15:28-29)

The prodigal son had sinned against the father but now it was evident that his sin was affecting his brother too, because the other half of the father's wealth belonged to the other brother. And the father was giving the sinful, repented son further access to the assets of the farm that had previously belonged to him when the sinful brother left. The sinful brother already received his half of the farm when he left.

> *His son said to him, Father, I have sinned against both heaven and you, and I am no longer worthy of being called your son. But his Father said to the servants, Quick! Bring the finest robe in the house and put it on him. Get a ring for his finger and sandals for his feet.* (Luke 15:21-22)

A family ring was like a credit card in those days and nice robes were hard to come by. The brother had his eye on both and now they were going to his sinful brother who already blew his half of the inheritance. He was not going to forgive him.

If the brother had forgiven him like the father had, he could have gone into the party and had a good time and hugged his brother. His staying outside wasn't going to make any difference; he would be the one suffering in the cold with no party food and drink. It was the father's ranch, and he was giving it to his brother whether he joined in or not.

There are many *other brothers* in church today when a son returns – don't be one of them. The hardest and heavier part of forgiveness has been done, and you are left with the easier part. Make the move to do the easier part and move closer to God when you do.

#25
Winning and Losing

Most Christians are not going to quit believing in Jesus when they lose a battle. Many will just quit serving God.

Eventually every human being on the planet will lose a battle to Satan, or it will look like a loss.

In the war to honor God and further His kingdom every person will experience what may look like a loss to themselves or to others, but there is never a loss when what you attempt to do is to glorify and honor God. If you take away the lens you see things through, there is no loss. God is a Sovereign God and if the results that come from the effort of someone who loves Him is always good, then there can be no loss

> *And we know that all things work together for the good to them that love God and are called according to His purpose.* (Romans 8:28)

The disciples thought the cross was a loss because they interpreted the results as such by what they saw and experienced. They took ownership of the loss rather than leaving the event in the hands of God and letting Him determine whether it was a loss or not. They quit serving God as disciples and went back to being fisherman. The same thing will happen to you when you start deciding what is lost and what isn't.

There will always be things that appear to be a loss when you fight the good fight for Jesus. The fact of the matter is the death of Jesus was a loss on Friday. He was dead by all appearances. It was game, set, and match. The people who stood by on that hill didn't make up the fact that Jesus was dead when they took Him down from the cross; He was dead, and He wasn't pretending. His death was physical, and it was real. They had killed the Messiah and there was no way to spin that into something positive. But that was man's reality, not God's reality. God was moving things into the win column and the people could not perceive the changes taking place in the spiritual world that would soon affect the physical in a way they could see.

God was changing the whole world's system of salvation in secret, and they couldn't see it until Sunday when Jesus was no longer dead but alive! This was God making the cross a win and not a loss. He did this by the mighty power of Jesus Christ without the help from any man, and He is still changing what looks like losers into winners for those who will believe.

> *Three days later, when David and his men arrived home at their town of Ziklag, they found that the Amalekites had made a raid into the Negev and Ziklag; they crushed Ziklag and burned it to the ground. They had carried off the women*

> *and children and everyone else but without killing anyone. When David and his men saw the ruins and realized what had happened to their families, they wept until they could weep no more. David's two wives, Ahinoam and Jesreel and Abigail, the widow of Nabal from Carmel, were among those captured. David was now in great danger because all of his men were very bitter about losing their sons and daughters, and they began to talk of stoning him. But David found strength in the Lord his God (*1 Samuel 30:1-6)

When you're losing something of great value it's okay to be distressed, but you shouldn't make the final call on the situation until God has His say. David inquired of the Lord, sharpened his sword, and got back to doing what he was born to do.

> *David and his men rushed in among them and slaughtered them throughout the night and the entire next day until evening. None of the Amalekites escaped except 400 young men who fled on camels. David got back everything the Amalekites had taken, and he rescued his two wives. Nothing was missing; small and great, son or daughter, or anything else that had been taken. David brough everything back. He also recovered all the flocks and herds, and his men drove ahead other livestock. This plunder belongs to David! They said.* (1 Samuel 30:17-20)

David recovered everything, lacked nothing, and took the spoils which means they were better off after the tragedy than before. The loss was turned into a win.

Your enemy is not human, and it does not matter how many times you put him down – he keeps getting up and coming back for more. Sometimes it seems only natural to think that after beating someone down so many times, at some point they would stay down. This enemy is not natural, it is a supernatural enemy, and we err when we get the idea that a given battle is won and the situation is now *handled*. It is never over until we see Jesus in heaven. If you know this is true then there are not so many highs and lows, and the danger of quitting that comes with them. If you stay in the fight mode, you can always be high and ready no matter what is happening around you.

It takes time, sometimes a lifetime, to see what we thought was lost was actually gained. When you lay everything at the feet of Jesus and you feel His hand on your head, you'll know everything has already been won.

So many people would rather never have a loss. No heartaches or setbacks is what they are after, but these things come to the one who walks with God. Trust God and leave the judgement of what is a loss and what is a win to Him.

Paul says: *To live is Christ and to die is gain.* (Philippians 1:21)

There are those who live this verse and those who wish they could, but one thing is for sure: once you get to the point where the things of this world no longer hold any value to you—including your next breath—there is nothing you can't do. You become a very dangerous individual to the kingdom of darkness and the battle will be brought to bear upon you and whatever God has called you to do. You will move in the might and the Spirit of the Living God, and what looks like a win or a loss will mean nothing to you because the outcome of any circumstance will be labeled by God and will be of no concern to you.

#26
The Chosen from The Called

It is a blessing to be part God's Plan.

Many are called but few are chosen (Matthew 22:14)

The chosen are selected from the called. God's plan is to move His chosen vessels in position to advance His plan on the earth and to further His kingdom. It is an honor to be part of a plan that He put together a long time ago.

You didn't choose me. I chose you. I appointed you to go and produce lasting fruit, so that the Father will give you whatever you ask for, using my name. (John 15:16)

Even before He made the world, God loved us and chose us in Christ to be holy and without fault in His eyes. (Ephesians 1:4)

But we are bound to give thanks always to God for you, brothers beloved of the Lord, because God hath from the beginning chosen you to salvation through sanctification of the Spirit and belief of the truth (2 Thessalonians 2:13)

No man that wars entangles himself with the affairs of this life; that he may please Him who hath chosen him to be a soldier. (2 Timothy 2:4)

There is a boatload of scripture that says you were chosen. Why is it so important that it is repeated in so many different scriptures and in different ways? Because being chosen is humbling knowledge when you realize you were chosen before you did anything. And being humble is what you need to succeed in the mission God gave you.

Being chosen is only a blessing if you choose to humble your heart and prepare yourself to participate. How can you tell if God has chosen you to be a part of His plan to further the kingdom? The Holy Spirit will draw you toward a thing, and many times you'll be the only one who can see it. Often the best indicator is immediate trouble before or after you move on the gumption from the Holy Spirit to do what He's called you to do.

There is no evidence that God ever used anybody on this earth to fulfill His plan and bring Him honor and glory who did not have to face multiple problems that could only be solved by Him. If God's only Son Jesus had to face multiple problems, then you will face them too. Jesus accomplished His mission because He never stopped looking to His Father in heaven for wisdom and strength. You will accomplish the plan God has for you by doing the same thing.

There is good news and bad news. The bad news is that the trials and trouble are here. The good news is that the trials and troubles are here. You cannot progress in faith trusting God if there is no opposition, trials, or trouble. Now that the opposition is here it is time to move though them. The greater the opposition you face the greater the work that needs to be done.

Some people in the Bible actually went looking for trouble that would glorify God because they were aware of the call on their life and wanted to get things going when the opportunity presented itself. If you're feeling called of God and want to be chosen by Him, you'd best abandon any thoughts of pride and insecurity and realize that you are nothing without Him and everything with Him. The Word says:

God resists the proud and gives grace to the humble (James 4:6)

You can't afford to have God's resistance if what you are trying to do requires His help.

There is a perfect example in the Bible that demonstrates how God chooses someone. Two brothers who saw the same problem. One saw opportunity and the other saw fear and unbelief in God's ability.

In 1 Samuel 16:6 the prophet Samuel went to the house of Jesse to anoint one of his sons to be king. The meeting took place in secret because King Saul would have killed them all if he knew what they were doing. The scripture says that Samuel saw one of the brothers, Eliab, and thought *surely the Lord has chosen this guy because he was big strong like King Saul*. But the Lord said:

> *But the Lord said to Samuel, don't judge by his appearance or height, for I have rejected him. The Lord doesn't see things the way you see them. People judge by the outward appearance, but the Lord looks at the heart.* (1 Samuel 16:7)

In order for Eliab to be rejected he first had to be considered. Very much like the chosen being selected from the called. Everyone is called to come to the banquet, but only some answer the call. Of those who answer the call, very few are chosen. What was it about Eliab that caused God to reject him? We will see later in this story.

Many people say *I don't know what God has for me to do* but it never occurs to them that maybe God is waiting for them to show Him what's in their heart to do. Maybe God wants to see if they will step out to honor His name without being asked or told what to do.

David was chosen by God and anointed to be king and it wasn't long before what was in his heart came out. David was sent to the Israeli's camp where thousands of soldiers camped out, paralyzed in fear of the giant Goliath. David was supposed to take food to his brother Eliab, and he was never told by God to fight Goliath. As David began to ask questions about the reward for killing the giant, and asking why this giant was allowed to profane the Living God, we see the reasons why God had earlier rejected Eliab at his father Jesse's house.

If there was one guy who should have stood up for David wanting to fight Goliath, it was Eliab. He was the only one who knew David had been anointed by Samuel in secret to be king of Israel. If Eliab had any faith in God or God's prophet, he would have known that David couldn't be killed until he was king. Not only was Eliab faithless, but he was also full of pride and jealousy which came from his own insecurities and fear. He attacked David for wanting to kill the giant because it would expose their cowardice and make them all look bad.

If you are to be chosen from the called you should expect a life event that will require faith and courage from you that will separate you from the pack and you best be ready for the opportunity when it comes. As it's been said, *Life is a River and not a Lake.* If you hesitate, the chance to step up may pass you by and you won't get it back.

There is no shrinking back from the destiny that God has for you. The only way you get there is to follow what God has put in your heart and trust Him to bring it to pass. The only guy in that camp who should have supported David was his older brother Eliab, and he didn't. Think about what could have been written about Eliab in the Bible if he had supported his brother David. There would still be sermons today about what a great example he was as an armor bearer or one who stood with his brother in the heat of the battle in faith and courage, but instead there is never another word mentioned about Eliab.

Eliab is only a footnote to a guy who had it all and used what he had to accomplish nothing.

Choose the path of David, keep following the Lord and know that you've been chosen for a work that only you can do and nothing will harm you until God's plan is fulfilled in your life. Don't be disappointed or discouraged if there are Christian brothers who don't support what you want to do; you're in good company.

#27
Flip Side

The promises of God are *Yes* and *Amen*. There are a thousand verses in the Bible that demonstrate how God stands beside someone who will believe in Him and His Word. The Bible is full of stories that illustrate people stepping up to face incredible odds and, with God's help, overcame danger and death to obtain victory and bring God glory.

There are only a few stories in the Bible where a person is advised to use restraint. God owns everything and so He rarely defends anything. God moves mainly in the offense, and you can see this by the things He says in His Word, and the things those who follow Him do in His Word.

Many Christians have a few "go to" verses in the Bible they use for justifying doing nothing. It isn't that the verses are not true and accurate and part of the Word of God; it's just that people use the verses to claim doing nothing is of God when they are being called to do something. They hide behind the verses that are meant for certain people in certain circumstances, and yet they claim the verses multiple times to justify doing nothing when God is calling them to move forward in faith.

A few of the versus you'll hear from people who do nothing are:

Where no council is, the people fall but in the multitude of councilors is safety. (Proverbs 11:14)

Rather than do what God tells them, they want to keep talking and thinking and having meetings about doing it. Another verse you hear all the time from people who do nothing is:

For which of you intending to build a tower doesn't sit down first and count the cost, whether or not he has enough to finish it? (Luke 14:28)

Sometimes God will call a person to start construction with no money. God can call a person to start with no money and, according to the scripture, they have considered the cost. They considered the cost, figured they had nothing, and figured God could do it! This verse is used by many who have no faith and will not move forward until they see all the funds and support needed to finish a task. They use this verse to justify doing nothing until they have the money in-hand.

For the reason mentioned above it is with hesitation that the Flip Side is written as this number #27 Devotion. However, there is a flip side to moving forward in faith and it is: *Waiting in faith*.

Some people will take the idea of waiting in faith and bend it for justification of living a faithless life. Others who are following and listening to the voice of the Holy Spirit know that there are times when waiting is the act of faith in God.

In Acts 27 Paul and his fellow prisoners were harbored at Fair Haven, which was an undesirable port that was exposed to the ocean without any cover from the wind. The time of year was the late fall, when the weather turned bad and most ships were in a harbor for a few months until better weather came. Because this was an exposed and undesirable harbor you can assume that not many boats planned to harbor there for months so it probably didn't have many boats and crews or restaurants and women, and there was probably not much of a night life. The prospect of staying there for months was not appealing.

The harbor at Phoenix was down the coastline and protected. It was known as a good place to harbor so there would be a lot of action and everything Fair Haven didn't have that a sailor could want.

Paul had a Word from the Holy Spirit that said everything they had, and maybe even their lives, would be lost if they took the journey. Paul didn't know whether or not they'd all die because the angel of the Lord had not appeared to him yet. In Acts 27:23 he told them that everything they had, the ship and the cargo would be lost if they chose to head out to sea.

If they chose to delay their trip and to wait in Fair Haven, they would have been waiting in faith based on their belief that what Paul said was from God. There is no indication that the man in charge was a Christian and it doesn't matter if he was or wasn't. When God calls a person to the flip side of faith to wait, they have to make a decision. Circumstances were driving the men to move when they shouldn't have.

There will be times in your life when waiting is not something you want to do and there will always be circumstances that will drive you to move when you shouldn't. If the sailors knew they'd be swimming for their lives in a cold, stormy ocean with a sinking ship behind them, the dull unprotected harbor of Fair Haven would look pretty good.

So, how can we miss the shipwrecks and still walk in faith? The answer is easy to say and harder to do: spend time in the Word, and in prayer, and follow what the Holy Spirit puts on your heart and then confirms with an open door when it is time to move. Until then take the *Flip Side of Faith*. Wait in faith and never use verses in the Bible to hide or justify fear.

We are all human and there will be times when we miss what God says, but if our goal is to glorify and bring honor to God, He will be with us wherever we find ourselves. If you are a doer for Christ then the flip side of faith is the hardest side to live on, but every servant of God has had to live there from time to time. The flip side of faith is not such a bad place to be if you compare it to where you'll be when you move outside of God's plan for your life.

#28
The Next Morning

The next morning, as agreed, Jonathan went out into the field and took a young boy with him to gather arrows. (1 Samuel 20:35)

David was alone for a couple of nights before *the next morning* hiding in a field. He was a wanted man with a death warrant from the king and more likely than not he probably spent the time hoping in prayer that he was going to be able to go back to the palace and join his wife and friends. David's future was at stake and the things going on around him didn't make any sense. He'd done nothing wrong. He had to be praying that God would somehow straighten things out.

David fled Naioth in Ramah and found Jonathan. "What have I done? He exclaimed. "What is my crime? How have I offended your father that he is so determined to kill me?" (1 Samuel 20:1)

David and Jonathan agreed to meet after Jonathan had a chance to talk with his dad the king. What was happening to David made even less sense to Jonathan, and he didn't believe that David had any reason to leave the palace or run from the king.

David was hoping for a positive sign from Jonathan the *next morning* to show that things had changed and that his world could return to normal.

All through the long days and nights hiding in the field he probably ran a hundred scenarios in his mind trying to figure out what he had done wrong and what he could do to set things right. No doubt he thought of his wife Michal and her warm bed at the palace.

From all the indicators David should have had high hopes and great faith toward a positive outcome from the meeting the *next morning*. Jonathan told David that he knew everything his dad was planning because his dad told him everything even to the smallest detail; he insisted there was no problem between David and King Saul.

Most of us tend to bend the Word we get from God to match what we desire. Instead of leaving the palace and hitting the road, which David knew in his heart was the path to take because of the circumstances, he hung around hoping he was wrong and hoping for a better outcome.

There were many reasons to give him hope for a positive outcome from the meeting with Jonathan on that *next morning*. That's why he waited but all the reasons in the world won't matter when God is moving you out. To the natural eye the following reasons he'd be allowed to stay were compelling:

1. He was anointed by Samuel to be king and he belonged in the palace.
2. He was the only one who could play the harp and bring peace to the king.
3. His best friend was the king's son.
4. The king's daughter loved him.
5. He married the king's daughter and was part of the king's family
6. He knew he had done nothing wrong
7. David was a mighty warrior who could defend Saul and Israel.

As the story goes in 1 Samuel 20: 35-42 the above reasons didn't change what God was doing. The outcome of the meeting wasn't what David was hoping for.

Jonathan had given it his best shot and actually risked his life to reason with his jealous Father,

Then Saul hurled his spear at Jonathan, intending to kill him. So at last Jonathan realized that his father was really determined to kill David. (1 Samuel 20: 33)

There was no reasoning with Saul. Despite all the reasons that said he should be going back to the palace, David wasn't going back. In spite of the truth presented to Saul, David would not be heading back to the palace. The *next morning's* meeting brought bad news and not what David wanted to hear. The message to David was, "Move on or die!"

When you've been somewhere for a while and you know the people and the routines it can be difficult to be uprooted. Sometimes it may be a church family or ministry that is the only thing that you have ever known. You may not face a physical death by staying like David, but there will be a death to your ministry if you stay when God is calling you to leave.

At this point following the *next morning's* meeting David did not complain or begin to recite the reasons why this shouldn't be happening to him. He didn't shout that he had done nothing wrong. David did not defend his actions, or call Saul an unfaithful king. He didn't say that he would fight with the king to take his rightful place. David took the outcome of the *next morning's* meeting as a sign from God. David hoped that truth and justice would prevail for his cause and that he could head back to the palace, but when Jonathan's boy ran past the arrows, he knew what he had to do if he was going to continue his destiny with God.

When you are faced with circumstances that make no sense and you negotiate and plan meetings to set things right and they go the other way from the logical conclusion you hoped and prayed for, it's time to Leave or Die.

David had done nothing wrong. He was where the prophet said he should be, he had people who loved him there and everybody thought he was a great guy—except one man. David couldn't figure out why this was happening. Maybe you can't figure out why you're going through what you're going through either. When God allows the *next morning* meeting to go bad after planning, prayer, and preparation, it's time to go.

David would never see his best friend Jonathan again. He would spend many years on the run from dark cave to dark cave before he would come back to the palace, but he never gave up hope in God's plan for his life. David wasn't sure how God would turn things around for him, but he knew God would.

Please let my parents stay here until I know what God is going to do for me (1 Samuel 22:3)

If there were times that David didn't know how or what God would do for him to fulfill His Word to him, then there will be times that you won't know how God is going to turn things around for you either.

Those who have a destiny in Christ will not spend their whole life enjoying the niceties of life in the palace. David was not able to occupy the throne of Israel as he was promised early in his life, but God made him king at the right time when David was ready later in life. Anyone who has the courage and faith to follow David's example when the doors close to leave the palace will experience the same victory coming back later to the palace or the place you belong that God has called you to.

In the end you'll be able to say what David said in his final Psalm:

I will exalt you, my God and King and praise your name forever and forever. (Psalm 145:1)

#29
Straight Lines

Because God is God with a capital *G,* He can do whatever He wants, whenever He wants. He is the Potter in a very large pottery barn and the totality of all things which are fashioned by Him have no ability to reach out from the clay and guide His hands. Many people think that who they are is mere chance, like the face of a stone that is shaped by the wind and the rain. That may be true in some instances, but God controls the wind and the rain, so you find yourself right back where you started with God, doing whatever He wants whenever He wants.

When God decides to do move, He could move in a straight line if He wanted. We have established that He can do anything, anytime, but He rarely does move in a straight line. Many people who are called of God to a specific task have the mistaken impression that because God desires something to be done, He will arrange for a straight line—a direct path for someone to travel on to accomplish that thing He wants done. By mistaking a straight line as evidence of being in God's will, many people have missed the call on their life and their destiny. Are there times of a straight line being a part of God's will? Yes, but it is rare. In the Word there are multiple accounts of people being led by a series of short lines and turns from point to point before arriving at the intended destination. If we use God's Word as a template, we can see how He moves in the lives of those He chose to use, and maybe we won't get confused or discouraged. We won't think we are out of His will when He moves the same way in our lives without a straight line.

God says what He is going to do before He does it. He has been doing that for thousands of years and He is the only One who can do that accurately.

Many people and their false religions with their poser God's have tried to speak to the future, but they have all failed. They've had to change their theology when their claims to the future didn't turn out the way they said. Jehovah God tells everybody, including the eternal spirits from hell, what He is going to do and lets them try to stop Him. And he laughs at their attempts.

But the one who rules in heaven laughs. The Lord scoffs at them (Psalms 2:4)

Two of the reasons God doesn't move in a straight line are:

1) If God were to move in a straight line it would be way too easy for His enemy to put up roadblocks and build pits for His servants to fall into along the way. God says what He is going to do and then

He conceals certain details so that His enemies have a hard time figuring out how He is going to do it. Can God blow through a roadblock and continue in a straight line? Sure, He can, but most of the time he creates a side road that no one considered.

2) When God moves in ways that only He knows about, His servants have to trust and rely on Him, and that builds their faith. When servants have faith in God, they are able to please Him.

And it is impossible to please God without faith. Anyone who wants to come to Him must believe that God exists and that he rewards those who sincerely seek Him (Hebrews 11:6)

One example of God moving from point to point rather than a straight line is when Jesus really wanted to have one last meal before His crucifixion with His disciples. He didn't give the address of the house and the name of the owner where the last supper would take place, instead the Word says:

So Jesus sent two of them into Jerusalem with these instructions: As you go into the city, a man carrying a pitcher of water will meet you follow him. At the house he enters, say to the owner, The Teacher ask: Where is the guest room where I can eat the Passover meal with my disciples? He will take you upstairs to a large room that is already set up. That is where you should prepare our meal. (Mark 14:13-15)

If Jesus had given the address of the last supper house and the owner's name to all 12 disciples, they would have all planned a *straight line* journey from where they were to where they were going. Judas could have revealed the location to the Pharisees and there would have never been a last supper. Jesus thought it was important to have one last meal and to show the disciples something about humility as He washed their feet. He wanted to give Judas one last chance to change his course. None of that would have taken place if Jesus had not thrown a few curves on how to get to the house.

There are many, many examples of how God moves His servants from place to place to accomplish His purposes. When it came time for the most important event on the planet to take place, God chose Mary and Joseph to fulfill what God said He was going to do thousands of years earlier:

He will strike your head and you will strike His heel. (Genesis 3:15)

Some scholars believe there are more than 300 prophecies about Jesus, the coming Messiah, in the Old Testament. Suffice it to say that every demon in hell knew the Messiah and the Savior of the world was coming for a long time before He got here. God's enemies were prepared to do anything to stop His arrival.

What God did to Joseph and Mary and His own Son living inside Mary was move them around in a way that resembled anything but a straight line. Joseph had four dreams that moved him in a jagged line to fulfill prophesy and preserve the life of God's Son. Joseph and Mary traveled back and forth and side to side from Bethlehem to Egypt to Israel to Nazareth to fulfill God's plan that they were a part of.

The first course of action for Joseph started out with him walking away quietly from the Marriage to Mary and the whole bad scene in Matthew 1:19.

His second course change came when he was told to stay with Mary, and he did (Mathew 1:24)

The third leg of the journey was to get up and go to Egypt as described in Matthew 2:14.

The fourth change up came in Matthew 2:20 when Joseph was told to go back to Israel.

The fifth time for a course deviation came when he was told to go to Galilee in Mathew 2:22.

Joseph followed the path that God laid out before him to protect Mary and Jesus. An unmarried woman who was pregnant in those days was stoned to death. Joseph made changes to his path that kept him from traveling a straight line to Galilee, but those changes allowed the fulfillment of many prophesies including:

A virgin will conceive: Isaiah 7:14 Isaiah 8:8-10 / Matthew 1:22

Messiah born in Bethlehem: Micah 5:2 / Matthew 2:5

Called my son out of Egypt: Hosea 11:1 /Matthew 2:14

The Messiah will be a Nazarene: Isaiah 11:1 Matthew 2:23

In all of the instructions Joseph received from God, there is not one recorded word of Joseph ever complained or interjected what he wanted to do. If Joseph wanted to be anything other than a faithful and obedient servant, he would have been a very unhappy guy, but it is evident by his words and actions that he was a faithful servant. He did much to fulfill the prophecy of God's Word.

Joseph isn't given much credit compared to Mary, but without Joseph Mary would never have made it to Bethlehem. She would have been stoned coming out of the gate. The love Joseph had for Mary and his willingness to follow God's path regardless of the direction made it possible for Joseph to follow a path that was anything but straight.

There are many people who equate a straight path with being in the will of God, and that's a big mistake. Some people believe that God will do for them what He did not do for His own Son, and what His own Son would not do for His own disciples. God has his reasons for how and when He moves. Trust Him and follow the line even when it seems to be going in the wrong direction. Let your love for people and your obedience to God lead you to the place of advancing the kingdom and don't be concerned if there are no straight lines on the path to your destination. The jagged edge on a jagged road is how a servant lives who brings glory to his God

Then he told them, go into all the world and preach the good news to everyone (Mark 16:15)

#30
One Day

In the first verse of the nineth chapter of the book of Luke, Dr. Luke starts out by saying *One Day,* before he starts to tell the story of what happened that day. The events that were about to take place on this particular day would reveal how God's power was designed to flow through His servants.

Although Dr. Luke was not a disciple, he was led by the Holy Spirit to interview and talk to those who were with Jesus and record the events. His account and the words he used to describe the events are recorded to help us know Jesus and walk with Him many centuries later.

When Luke says *one day* it was a day different from all the others. The events that were about to take place were not described as happening over a few days or weeks. The events that took place did not happen over the course of the year, it happened on *one day*.

During the days leading up to this *one day* the disciples had been traveling and listening to Jesus and watching Him perform miracles. Their role was one of listening, watching and learning. They were first-hand eyewitnesses to what the power of God could do but they had no firsthand experience of moving in the Spirit.

The disciples observed the mighty power that flowed from the voice and the touch of Jesus, but it wasn't a power they knew or understood, and that's why they said:

Who is this man that even the wind and the waves obey Him? (Luke 8:25)

They had seen the servant of a powerful roman officer healed by just the word of Jesus in Luke 7:7, and a widow's son raised from the dead when He touched the boy's coffin and called him to life in Luke 7:14-15. The disciples saw Jesus put all of them in harm's way to cross the Sea of Galilee at night to reach just one demon possessed man in Luke 8:26-39.

When Jesus asked the disciples, "Who touched me?" in Luke 8:45 they had no idea why He would ask such a question. They did not understand what He was talking about because there were multitudes of people pressing in on Him and touching Him. They were oblivious to the concept of spiritual power leaving Him when being touched, by the faith of someone. They had no experience of the Spirit moving from within them to minister to others.

Everything was about to change on this *One Day* that Dr. Luke records. The disciples were about to find out from first-hand experience what it was to move in the Spirit instead of just watching someone else do it. This day was going to be unlike any other day that they had lived in their entire life. The Bible says:

> *One day Jesus called together his twelve Disciples and gave them the power and authority to cast out demons and to heal every disease. Then He sent them out to tell everyone about the Kingdom of God and to heal the sick.* (Luke 9:1-2)

There is no indication that the disciples knew or expected that this *one day* would show up when it did. There was no warning and Jesus never said at an earlier point that next week or next month you'd better be ready because I'm going to give you power and authority to go out and advance the kingdom. This *one day* came out of nowhere and it was time to start pushing the kingdom. They had all seen the power and been a part of watching, but now it was time to apply what they saw and heard in their own lives.

The disciples wouldn't know about the power and authority that was given to them by Jesus until they went out to further the kingdom. There was no evidence of that power until they applied it for the purpose He intended. The word Jesus used for the twelve disciples when He called them together before He sent them out in the above verse Luke 9:1 was disciple or *mathetes* in the Greek, which means *learner*. When the twelve returned from telling the people about the Kingdom of God and healing the sick in Luke 9:10 the word used for the group was *apostles* or *apostolos* in the Greek which means *a messenger or one who sent with orders*.

The twelve went from learners to being sent to spread what they learned to further the kingdom of God. They were given power and authority to further the kingdom of God and not their own kingdom. The fact that they were called *messengers* means that they were successful in giving the message. Anyone who is given the power and authority by Jesus Christ to further the kingdom will be successful in doing that.

A rifle and bullets do nothing while the bullets sit on a shelf and the rifle is locked in a safe. Bullets are made to be shot but as long as the bullets are separate from the rifle, they do nothing. You can hold the bullets in your hand without the rifle and throw them at something, but they won't do much damage. The power and authority of the Spirit is not given to someone so that they can have goosebumps or manipulate things for their own benefit. It is given to enable someone to go out and further the kingdom of God and reach a lost and dying world.

Your voice to tell people about the kingdom of God and heal the sick is the rifle. The power and authority of the Spirit is the bullet that moves through the rifle. A rifle is useless without bullets and so are your efforts to further the kingdom and heal the sick without power and authority. Many people are just throwing bullets without a rifle because they seek the power and authority of the Spirit to further their own agenda. Others, like Judas, are given the power and authority and then they get twisted. Judas was one of the twelve who experienced the power and authority to further the kingdom and heal the sick, but he had his own agenda. He held the bag of money and entertained the enemies of the kingdom, betraying the Lord and his brothers.

When your *one day* comes, be ready! When the opportunity to further the kingdom and pray for someone to be healed is presented to you, take it and let the power and authority from the Holy Spirit change you from a disciple to an apostle as you feel the bullet of the Holy Spirit surge through you.

#31
Walking Through

The Word says:

One Sabbath day as Jesus was walking through some grain fields, his disciples began breaking off heads of grain to eat. (Mark 2:23)

Jesus was walking through some grain fields and his disciples began breaking off heads of grain to eat. The custom of the day was for farmers to leave the corners of a field unharvested so that the poor could take the harvest from the corners of the field and have something to eat. Most people think that Jesus and His disciples were taking advantage of this custom of unharvested corners to get something to eat. The pharisees were saying that Jesus was breaking the law by working on the Sabbath. The point of the story was to show that Jesus is Lord of everything, including the

Sabbath, but there is another, less obvious, point that holds a key to unlocking God's blessings in your life.

If the disciples were in fact walking around the corners of the field gleaning wheat that was left for the poor, the Bible would have said that was what they were doing, but it doesn't say that. The Word says they were *walking through* the field. Also, it is not likely that Jesus and His disciples would be taking food away from the poor by picking wheat that was left for them.

The corners of the field were purposely left open by the landowner for the poor to have some food so anyone found picking wheat in those corners would not be trespassing on the owner's land. This ancient custom of leaving the corners open for the poor did not give license for the poor or anyone else to trespass, to go past the corners and enter the rest of the owner's field.

Jesus never committed one sin, or we would all be toast. He was a Lamb without blemish and that is how He was able to conquer the grave. His sinless life is what guarantees that we shall also conquer the grave. If Jesus *walked through* a man's field and His disciples took the grain that was meant for that man's profit, then they would have been breaking two laws. Number one they would have been trespassing, and number two, they would be stealing grain from the owner of the field.

Because Jesus did rise from the dead and come back from the grave, we know that neither of the above two laws were broken. The only way those laws could not have been broken was for Jesus to have had permission from the landowner to leave the road or pathway to *walked through* his field and let His disciples take some of his for-profit grain.

Does Jesus have permission to *walk through* your field? Many of us do things to help the less fortunate or poor and leave 10% or the corners of our field open for them. We tithe 10% of our income, which does not belong to us, and maybe give our old clothes to the mission. But what about the things that do belong to us? What about the bulk of what we own or the 90% of the field that is not set aside for the poor? Does Jesus have permission to *walk through* your field—your business, your real estate, your bank account—and take what He needs for His servants?

The needs of God's servants will be met by someone. There are many fields of grain beside the roads that Jesus and His servants are still walking today. Not every landowner will be asked by Jesus for permission to walk through their field and for them to do more than just leave open the corners of the field. The Holy Spirit will bring the opportunity for Jesus to walk through a specific person's field who God desires to bless.

The biggest mistake a person can make with their field is to think that God needs them and their field. Jesus can use any man's field and the fact that he is asking to *walk through* yours says that He has prepared blessings for you. You need to give Him permission to *walk through* your field so that according to His Word He can bless you. God does not operate outside of His Word and He will stay out of your field if you want Him to.

Pay attention to this unseen part of the story that reveals that Jesus is Lord of all including the Sabbath and understand that increase comes to those who are willing to give more than just the corners of their fields: God is looking for those who are willing to give Him permission to *walk through* their fields so that they can become part of the story of what God is doing in these last days.

> *Remember this, a farmer who plants only a few seeds will get a small crop. But the one who plants generously will get a generous crop. You must each decide in your heart how much to give. And don't give reluctantly or in response to pressure. For God loves a person who cheerfully gives. And God will generously provide all you need. Then you will always have everything you need and plenty left over to share with others. For God is the one who provides seed for the farmer and then bread to eat. In the same way, He will provide and increase your resources and then produce a great harvest of generosity in you. Yes, you will be enriched in every way so that you can always be generous. And when we take your gifts to those who need them, they will thank God* (2 Corinthians 9: 6-11)

> *Be not deceived; God is not mocked; whatever a man sows that shall he also reap.* (Galatians 6:7)

#32
Storm's Coming

If you are where God wants you to be and you're doing what He wants you to do then there is a storm coming. A thunderstorm of blessings is directed toward the person who is walking uprightly before God.

For the Lord God is our sun and our shield. He gives us grace and glory. The Lord will withhold no good thing from those who trust in you. (Psalms 84:11)

It is a very good thing when a rainstorm shows up to bring life to dry ground. God says He will open the windows of heaven for a person who does not withhold their tithes and offerings.

Should people cheat God? Yet you have cheated me! But you ask, What do you mean? When did we ever cheat you? You have cheated me of the tithes and offerings due me. Bring all the tithes into the storehouse so there will be enough food in my temple. If you do, says the Lord of Heaven's Armies, I will open the windows of heaven for you. I will pour out a blessing so great you won't have enough room to take it in! Try it! Put me to the test! (Malachi 3:8-10)

God's Word describes the approaching blessings that are coming your way as blessings that come from an open window in the sky. When the sky opens its the result of a storm. If you have done what God has asked, then it is only a matter of time before you are going to be hit by the storm. God either is who He says He is, or He's not. His Word is either true, or it's not.

There are basically two groups of people who are waiting on the storm of blessings. A group who tithes and one who doesn't. As you can probably guess, one group is much larger than the other. The smaller group are people who believe what God says and they act on those beliefs. This smaller group looks out at the horizon every morning to see if there are any clouds. Their promise is secure, and they patiently wait for what they know is coming

Patience endurance is what you need now, so that you will continue to do God's will. Then you will receive all that He has promised you. (Hebrews 10:36)

The larger group with sticky fingers also looks towards the horizon each morning. They hope a storm of blessing is coming but they know inside that there is no storm on the way, and they act accordingly by keeping what belongs to God. This larger group of non-tithing thieves hope that God isn't paying attention to what they do with His money, especially when they need something from God. The smaller group is thankful that God is paying attention to their giving and they keep an eye out for the coming storm.

God's promised blessings are to those who do what is pleasing to Him.

> *And we will receive from Him whatever we ask because we obey Him and do the things that please Him* (1 John 3:22)

A storm at sea cannot be stopped by any power on earth. Neither can the blessings that are coming to those who have planted seed and followed the Word of God in faith. When the storm arrives and the windows of heaven open there is no stopping the rain until the amount of rain in the clouds has gone out, and so it will be with your blessings. Your blessings will continue until the amount that God has measured for you has been completely meted out. This measured amount will be determined by you, not God.

> *Remember this-a farmer who plants only a few seeds will get a small crop. But the one who plants generously will get a generous crop.* (2 Corinthians 9:6)

It may seem like a long time has passed as you have waited for the promised blessings, but they will surely come.

> *for the vision is yet for an appointed time, but at the end it will be fulfilled. If it seems slow in coming, wait patiently for it will surely take place it will not be delayed. (Habakkuk 2:3)*

What do you do when you know a big rainstorm is coming? When you know that the heavens are going to open up and dump inches of rain, you prepare!

Many people do not prepare for the abundant blessings from God. They expect the blessings of God to show up on a nice sunny day without much change taking place. Because of this error in judgement and lack of preparation many Christians do not survive the storm and the blessings of God. They are washed downstream or snowed under with the changes that take place. Suddenly they find themselves far above any of the old concerns for paying bills and the stress that came at the end of the month. After the storm they have options, and many are no longer desperate for the presence of God and they begin to worship God at their leisure. After the storm they can spend time thinking of ways to spend money instead of thinking of ways to find money, and it isn't long before the things of God are no longer a priority.

The Word says that the windows of heaven will open with blessings. Have you ever seen the windows of heaven open during a storm when it was nice and sunny? God's blessings are a two-edged sword and if you're not prepared your decisions after the storm can cut you deep. God's answers to your prayer and His faithfulness to His Word are wonderful, and yet those blessings can be used to take your focus off Christ if you let them. Money is not evil; it has no soul. The blessings of God can be used to build a house for hookers or a church house. It is up to the one who holds the increase to decide what to do with it.

Prepare yourself. There is a storm coming that you have been waiting for. This storm is intended to bless you, so let it be a blessing and stay a blessing by preparing yourself and your family. Check yourself to see that pride and envy is in line with the Word. Keep lust and coveting a good distance away from your thoughts. Put aside your anger issues knowing that you have done more to anger God that any person could ever do to you. And don't do anything after the storm of blessings arrives that you would not have done before it arrived.

You will be dealing with a different person after the storm arrives. This person will have access to things your old person didn't have, and this new person will want to partake in some of those new things. Don't do it! If you wouldn't go to that party before, don't go to it now. If you wouldn't take that weekend trip before the storm, don't take it now. If you would not watch that movie before, don't watch it now. If you wouldn't go to lunch with him or her before the storm, don't go to lunch with him or her now. If you'd let an offense go without being offended before the storm, don't be offended now.

This devotion is aimed at the smaller group who tithe and give offerings that have a storm of blessings on the way. They are the ones who will make a difference in the world for Christ, not the larger group with no power to do anything.

If you are part of the larger group with those sticky fingers you can change that in one minute. While reading this devotion the Holy Spirit has already told you how. It's up to you if you want to join the smaller group that is changing the world for Christ, but you are now forewarned. If you join the smaller group who trust God with their money, there's a *storm coming* and you'd best be ready for it.

#33
Lord of the Breaks

After 20 years on the run David was through running and he was ready to step into the role he was called to as king. You might think that after years of trials and battles to get to his calling, he'd have some peace when he finally arrived where he was supposed to be. But that wasn't the case. His first battle as king would come quickly as the Jebusites taunted and ridiculed him, saying that even the blind and lame could keep him from his calling to capture Jerusalem. (2 Samuel 5:6) They had no respect for him or his new position as king.

It is useful to observe how the events unfolded when David began to live the life that God said he would live as king. Many people think that when they finally arrive at the place that God has for them that everything will be peaches and cream. The problem with that thinking is it can work to tear down your faith in God and His calling on your life. If you have been expecting God to put you on a smooth road, when the road gets bumpy you can start thinking that this is not the road that God put you on. That thinking will steal your faith and then you're done.

David knew from experience that every position he held that was given to him by God would be challenged by an enemy. Whether it was a bear, a giant, or a king, there was always someone trying to take away what God had given him. Now that he was king, he expected no less.

The forces of darkness will always try and take away what God has given you. The forces of darkness will always try to knock you out of where God has placed you. The devil has no ability to be in all places at all times. Only the Holy Spirit has that resume. If multiple resources from hell are being directed at you then whether you know it or not, God has something very significant for you to accomplish to further His kingdom. The greater the attack against you the greater importance of your calling.

There is no doubt that God loved David, just as there is no doubt that He loves you. If God didn't stop the attack when David stepped into his calling, then you can pretty much figure He is not going to stop the attack when you move into your calling. The good news is that He has given you His anointing, power and insight to defeat any attack that is sent to take you down if you will trust in God and follow the way He tells you to go.

As soon as David defeated one foe and captured the city of Jerusalem his old nemeses the Philistines came knocking.

> *When the Philistines heard that David had been anointed King of Israel, they mobilized all their forces to capture him*

> *but David was told they were coming, so he went into the stronghold.* (2 Samuel 5:17)

Don't think it strange or unusual to have to deal with a problem again after you thought it was handled. Sometimes a recurring problem can make you think that it is something that is going to take you down because it keeps coming back. This story and all stories of the Bible are written for learning and benefit to us

> *All scripture is given by inspiration of God, and is profitable for doctrine, for reproof, for correction, for instruction in righteousness* (2 Timothy 3:16)

David went to his stronghold and then defeated the enemy's plan to remove him from where God put him. Your stronghold is the Holy Spirit and the Lord Jesus Christ and when you go to them your results will be the same as David's.

The Bible tells us that David called the place after the battle with the Philistines *Baalperazim* or *Lord of the Breaks* (2 Sam 5:20.) He asked the Lord if He could defeat the Philistines and God said that he could, so David went at them head on with such force that he called the place the *Lord of The Breaks* or the Lord who comes bursting through with great force and great numbers. And yet in spite of being soundly defeated the Word says:

> *But after a while the Philistines returned again and spread out across the Valley of Rephaim.* (2 Samuel 5:22)

Why would the Philistines come back for more after being defeated so badly that David named the place

Baalperazim? Here's the short answer: because what you beat down yesterday sometime has to be beat down again today.

And why wouldn't David attack them the same way he had done before especially if the outcome was such a great victory and a rout of the enemy? Why would anyone think that waiting for the sound of soldiers' feet on top of the mulberry trees would be a good strategy for winning a battle? Nobody would, unless they believed that the battle was the Lord's and then it would make perfect sense to do whatever you heard God say to do. A person can say anything, but they do what they believe. David said he believed God and he did what God said to do.

Anyone who steps into a significant calling from God can expect some ridicule, an attack, and then another attack. If you operate from the stronghold you will prevail, if you follow man's ideas and your own wisdom you will fail.

#34
Corners

The beginning corners of a sail on a sailboat have different names. One is called a *clew*. The clew is reinforced with additional fabric and stitching to keep it from tearing. There is substantially more pressure on the corner of the sail that is attached to the boat than what the center of the sail experiences. The greater area of the sail has many feet of sail that can average out the force of the wind in the billow of the sheet, but the clew has all the force of the entire sail brought to bear upon a small corner piece of the sheet that can be measured in inches.

The Word says

The beginning of the gospel of Jesus Christ, the Son of God. (Mark 1:1)

The Greek word used the New Testament for *beginning* in this verse is *arche*, which mean beginning or origin. One description for the word is *beginning such as the corners of a sail.*

The beginning of the gospel is the Son of God, Jesus Christ. If Jesus Christ is not the Son of God, there is no gospel and there is no good news. Jesus, like the beginning or corner of a sail on a ship, is the most important part of the gospel. You can have the strongest and most beautiful sail in the world but without a clew, or corner, the sail is useless and the boat the sail is attached to is not going anywhere. Any person, church or religion that tries to navigate a path forward without Jesus is exactly the same; they are not going anywhere. When your trust in something other than Jesus you've lost your corners.

Jesus said:

The stone which the builders rejected has become the chief cornerstone. (Mark 12:10)

A stone building can't be built without cornerstones, and a chief cornerstone can anchor a whole building experiencing more stress and pressure than any other component of the entire structure. And just like a sail without a corner, a building without a cornerstone is useless.

Corners of a building and a sail are incredibly strong, which was part of Jesus's job description when He came to the earth to redeem mankind. Jesus is incredibly strong! The entire weight of the fulfillment of the law was upon Him and He charted the way forward for His church and His people by the shedding of His blood and coming back from the grave, If you lean on Him, he won't tear out or crumble when you do. He will lead you where you need to go, across oceans if that's what it takes, and He will establish you in your place without fear that what your building will collapse.

You can trust Jesus to get you where you need to be. A boat is not pushed by the sail, it is pulled. The Holy Spirit gently pulls and guides you where He wants you to go according to His plan and when there is a storm, He will lead you into port to wait it out. If you are feeling pushed and prodded to do something the chances are that you are not being led by the Holy Spirit.

A ship that has a sail with no corners is at the mercy of the wind and tide. You can turn the wheel and rudder to try navigating but it won't make any difference. Without the strength of the sail with corners to pull you on course you will not make your destination.

A building that stands during a storm has a solid foundation and cornerstones. If you've come through a storm and there is nothing left afterwards then your foundation wasn't based on Jesus being the Son of God. You can be the best and most knowledgeable contractor on earth making perfect rafter cuts and dead level walls, but your buildings will all collapse in a storm without a solid foundation and cornerstones.

Some people don't think they need corners or the strength of Jesus to guide or protect them. They point at their possessions as proof until a storm comes.

> *Anyone who listens to my teaching and follows it is wise, like a person who builds a house on a solid rock. Though the rain comes in torrents and the floodwaters rise and the winds beat against the house, it won't collapse because it is built on bedrock. But anyone who hears my teaching and doesn't obey it is foolish, like a person who builds a house*

on the sand. When the rains and floods come and the winds beat against the house, it will collapse with a mighty crash (Matthew 7:24-27)

If you need strength in your life turn to Jesus and get some corners.

#35
Come a Little Further

Then a leader of the local synagogue, whose name was Jairus, arrived. When he saw Jesus, he fell at His feet, pleading fervently with Him. My little girl is dying, he said Please come and lay your hands on her; heal her so she can live. Jesus went with him, and all the people followed crowding around Him. (Mark 5:22-24)

The most precious things to most of us in this world is our children. Jairus got the great news that Jesus had said okay to his request and his little girl was going to be okay. He was leading Jesus to his house because Jesus didn't know where he lived. Jairus was probably pressing Jesus to hurry up because she was dying. If you were around someone as famous as Jesus was with such a great multitude of people all shouting and wanting something from Him, your progress back to the house form the shoreline would be slow. The whole time you would be hoping that your little girl could hang on until you got there.

Then about halfway to the house everything stopped as some lady that was banned from the temple because she was ceremonially unclean touched Jesus. Another conversation that sounded crazy started as everything ground to a halt. Jesus realized at once that healing power had gone out from Him, so He turned around in the crowd and asked,

Who touched my robe? (Mark 5:30)

No one could figure out what Jesus was asking because to them it was impossible to tell who individually touched Him. To Jairus the fact that Jesus was asking a question that couldn't be answered meant a long delay, and more delays was the last thing he was hoping for. And now Jesus was starting a conversation with this woman who was poor and sick and banned from the temple.

Then the frightened woman, trembling at the realization of what happened to her, came and fell to her kneed in front of Him and told him what she had touched Him (Mark 5:33)

The thing about delays in getting what Jesus has promised is that they have a way of tearing down your faith. When a promise is given (and every Word of Jesus is a promise by virtue of the fact that He spoke it) we are very excited about what that promise means for our future, but as time goes by our hopes begin to dim when we don't see the promise fulfilled.

Jairus had gone down to the water's edge to meet Jesus and the disciples when they came into town.

There was no record of whether Jairus was a believer or not. He was desperate to save his daughter's life and he took what faith he had to Jesus. As Jairus struggled to keep it together and hold onto the words of Jesus, what he feared the worse happened

> *While he was still speaking to her, messengers arrived from the home of Jairus, the leader of the synagogue. They told him; your daughter is dead. There's no use troubling the Teacher now.* (Mark 5:35)

This was crushing news. Jairus had to have thought: *If it wasn't for these people and that crazy woman we'd have already been to my house and my daughter would be healed and alive.* Maybe he heard about the Roman centurion who told Jesus all he had to do was speak the word and his servant would be healed and there was no need for Jesus to even go to his house. Maybe he wished he had the faith of that centurion so he could have saved his little girl. When tragedy strikes there are a million things that go through your mind, but the biggest thing is fear.

When Jesus heard the report of the little girl dying His immediate concern was for Jairus. He knew His power was unlimited, so He wasn't worried about the girl, but he didn't want Jairus to lose what faith he had.

> *But Jesus overheard them and said to Jairus, don't be afraid. Just have faith* (Mark 5:36)

What did Jairus have to be afraid of? His daughter was already dead. The word for *afraid* in this verse is the Greek word: *phobeo* which means: *to put to flight by terrifying, to flee.*

Where was Jairus going to go? He wasn't going to physically run from his house and leave his 12-year-old girl who died, alone in the corner.

Jesus knew that Jairus would flee from faith in Him with the greater miracle that would now be needed to bring her back from the dead. Jesus was saying, "Don't run away from the faith you had when you came to me." This sheer terror was brought to bear on Jairus, and Jesus was saying, "Stay here with me in faith and don't run away to doubt and fear." Jesus was saying, "Come a little further with me. You trusted me this far, *come a little further* with me."

Whatever the trouble you face or whatever miracle you may need, Jesus says the same thing to you today: *come a little further* with me. Things may get worse as they often do while we wait on the Lord, but it only seems worse to us not Him. Whether or not you are an educated priest that can memorize the Torah or your education is one of hard knocks on the battlefield like the centurion, you must come to Jesus with what faith you have. And when you do, He will never turn you away.

> *All that the Father gives me shall come to me; and him that comes to me I will in no way cast out.* (John 6:37)

> *Come unto me, all you who labor and are heavy laden, and I will give you rest. Take my yoke upon you, and learn of me; for I am meek and lowly in heart; and you shall find rest for your souls. For my yoke is easy, and my burden is light.* (Matthew 11:28-30)

#36
Roof Wreckers

When Jesus returned to Capernaum several days later, the news spread quickly that He was back home. Soon the house where He was staying was so packed with people that there was no more room, even outside the door. While He was preaching God's Word to them, four men arrived carrying a paralyzed man on a mat. They couldn't bring him to Jesus because of the crowd, so they dug a hole through the roof above His head. Then they lowered the man on his mat, right down in front of Jesus (Mark 2:1-4)

The glaring question is what kind of people would keep a paralyzed man from Jesus? These people were in the presence of Jesus, who is the definition of love and caring for others, and they don't let a paralyzed man in to be healed? With four guys and a mat they were not hard to see but the people chose to block them out. The people in the house cared more for themselves than they did for this man, his friends, and his family.

When the paralyzed man was blocked from seeing Jesus, there is no record that the man or his four friends said anything. He didn't start yelling like some of the other people to get the attention of Jesus. The paralyzed man knew there was nothing he could do, but his friends were another story. They put action to their faith and started climbing stairs to the roof where they tore the roof apart to lower their friend down to the feet of Jesus. Everybody had to know what they were doing. Tearing a hole in the roof above where people are standing would send debris down on the heads of the people below, including Jesus. When the chunks of roof started landing on people below you can figure that the meeting below came to a halt and everybody had to be looking up at what was taking place.

Making a hole in the roof large enough to lower a man on a stretcher through it would take time and effort, and you could be sure that the owner of the house had to be trying to get up there to stop them from ruining his roof. There were probably only two guys tearing up the roof to make room for their buddy and the stretcher, the other two guys were posted up at the top of the stairs to fight off the homeowner and his friends who were coming up to stop them.

What's interesting is that Jesus knew what these four guys were doing and said nothing to stop them. As the debris began to fall and a small hole opened up, Jesus could have spoken to them before it got much bigger. Jesus could have spoken the word and healed their friend before they tore up more of the roof. He could have gone up there himself to heal the man and keep things from getting out of hand between the owner and the Roof Wreckers, but He didn't.

These guys were being kept out of the presence of Jesus and His healing power, and they were not going to take it laying down. Jesus let them run with what they wanted to do.

The Word says:

And from the days of John the Baptist until now the Kingdom of Heaven suffers violence, and the violent take it by force. (Matthew 11:12)

When Jesus talks about violence, he is talking about people with courage who are willing to take what He offers even if they have to fight to get it. He was talking about spiritual and physical violence. Most people who have given up a bad drug habit say that it was the fight of their life to get clean and follow the Lord.

It doesn't make sense to think that the removal of the roof from somebody's house without their permission would be a somber and quiet undertaking while everybody watched the debris fall in respectful silence. This event probably had lots of yelling and arm waving but Jesus didn't say anything, He just watched the four men's faith in action as some of them pulled and ripped through the roof and the others fought off the owner and his friends until the man was at His feet.

The first thing Jesus said before being asked for anything was

Seeing their faith, Jesus said the paralyzed man, My child, your sins are forgiven (Mark 2:5)

The paralyzed man's friends wanted to give him a better life and get him healed by Jesus, and they ended up getting him a much, much bigger gift. They brought him to the Man who gave him eternal life.

There are people today who are willing to take what Jesus has given them to a lost and dying world – by force if they must. Their monetary giving and gifts can only be described as courageous as it is far above and eclipses anything near 10% Their hearts are centered on praying for and reaching the lost, and they are constantly looking for ways to bring people to Jesus. They are like these Roof Wreckers, always talking about and imagining new ways of reaching the lost for Christ.

There is no room for excuses when seeking the lost and following Christ. Those who mean business don't debate the politeness of the scripture Matthew 8:22 or what it means

Let the Dead bury the dead. (Matthew 8:22)

They get it. They understand that nothing is more important than following Christ. And they do what they have to do to make Jesus and furthering His Kingdom a priority. Those who are dead to that understanding and life commitment can bury the dead.

Some of those who push the kingdom of God may be a little rough on the edges, and they may tear things up from time to time, but reaching the lost for Christ is all worth it to a Roof Wrecker.

#37
Half a Loaf

In Matthew 14:19 He told the people to sit down on the grass. Jesus took the five loaves and two fish, looked up towards Heaven, and blessed them. Then, breaking the loaves into pieces, He gave the bread to His disciples, who distributed it to the people.

If Jesus split the food up equally between the twelve disciples, each disciple would have had a half a loaf of bread and one-sixth of a fish. We can assume this because the disciples didn't say anything after Jesus prayed, saying that suddenly there was more food in the baskets. A miracle was needed as they headed out with a half a loaf and a small piece of fish to feed at least a thousand people each. The Word says there were 5,000 men plus women and children so there was easily over twelve thousand people gathered there.

It is important to recognize that the miracles of multiplied food took place after they left Jesus and went out to distribute the food.

When you find yourself in the place of needing a miracle, it is usually God that has allowed you to be in that place for one of two reasons. He is trying to teach you something, or He is bringing you to a place where He can make an adjustment and correct something in your actions or thinking. In either case He is going to bring a miracle in your life and that is the good news. The bad news is also that He is going to bring a miracle in your life and you're going to need it.

More often than not when a person needs a miracle it means that something is needed that only the supernatural can fulfill. And in such cases, there is usually a great degree of stress. There are two types of miracles that we can experience.

In one type of miracle the physical things around us can be altered and arranged supernaturally. Many people will call that a coincidence even though it is not. The other type of miracle take place when the physical elements around us are altered. Things are created or destroyed or changed before our eyes by the hand of God.

If a big cart filled with food happened to be driving by on the hilltop above the crowd and a rabbit ran by that spooked the horses pulling the cart and the cart flipped over raining fish and loaves on the crowd, that would be a miracle of the first kind. In the case of feeding over 5,000 people with a half loaf of bread and part of a fish is a miracle of the second kind.

Each disciple had a basket so that each disciple could see with their own eyes and feel with their own hands the provision and the miracle power of God to create something from nothing. Jesus could have kept all the food and handed it out to the disciples as it was multiplied from the one basket that the fish and loaves came in.

Instead of leaving the food in the original basket, Jesus purposely took a half loaf of bread and one-sixth of a fish and put it into each of the eleven other empty baskets leaving a half loaf and one-sixth of a fish in the original basket. Jesus could have taken 13 baskets and kept all the food that was being multiplied by miracle in His basket. The disciples could have gone up and down the hill filling their baskets from Jesus's basket, but He didn't do it that way. By breaking the food up into 12 baskets and giving each disciple their own basket Jesus was making each disciple an eyewitness to God's miraculous provision.

Instead of one miracle taking place in one basket in the hands of Jesus, there were 12 different miracles taking place in 12 different baskets to build the faith of 12 different men. Each man would have his very own story of what happened to their half loaf and piece of fish. Each disciple would have their faith increased by a miracle that was made personal to them.

Jesus still wants to put a half loaf in the basket you are carrying and send you out to experience His miracle of provision along the way, but most people won't move unless the basket is full before they go. Unfortunately, a full basket with no surprises is what many Christians require before stepping out to do what God tells them to do. That is why most people never experience any miracles in their life. The miracles they talk about are always miracle's that happened to somebody else. They have no witness of God's miraculous provision themselves.

The story of the 12 disciples feeding the 5,000 and again feeding the 4,000 would build their faith in God over the years when they remembered the power and provision of God. Experiencing miracles has a way of doing that.

We don't know how many loaves and fishes were created because the Word doesn't tell us, but it does tell us what was left over from both events. God wanted us to know what was left over after feeding the 5,000 and the 4,000 or He would not have included that information in His Word. Perhaps God wanted to encourage us thousands of years later by showing us that He has every detail of every event accounted for and that's why he included the leftover amounts.

There were 12 baskets filled with food that were left over after feeding the 5,000. The people in this group were mostly Jews and it could be a way to say that Jesus was enough for the 12 tribes of Israel. He filled the requirements of the law and He would satisfy their needs for a Messiah.

> *For all of God's promises have been fulfilled in Christ with a resounding yes! And through Christ, our Amen which means yes ascends to God for His Glory* (2 Corinthians 1:20)

There were 7 baskets left over when Jesus fed the 4,000 and the crowd there was mostly Gentiles. In the Bible, 7 is the number representing perfection. There were 7 baskets left over that could be a way to show that Jesus was a perfect redeemer and that they would need nothing else to be saved except for faith in Him.

> *But when that which is perfect is come, then that which is in part shall be done away.* (1 Corinthians 13:10)

#38
Doors

When you see a door without hinges it is usually being used as part of a wall. It is either nailed or screwed into place and is permanently shut. Most doors have hinges that allow them to open and close. It is useful to remember that hinges swing both ways, and when a door is closed it doesn't necessarily mean that it is locked.

Many Christians come to closed doors and walk the other way without ever knocking, assuming the door is locked. If there is something on the other side of the door that they want, they reason that it would be easier to stop wanting what was there than to risk knocking on the door and then have to deal with the disappointment of the door remaining shut. This kind of emotional protection will cost you multiplied blessings from God that wait on the other side of the door in front of you. Some doors take more faith to knock on than others, but if you never knock, you'll never know what God had planned for your life.

We all progress in life through a series of doors. On the day of your birth you pass through an open door to life on earth, and on the day of your death you pass through an open door to eternal life in Heaven. In the area in between there are many doors. The ones you choose to knock on will decide what you do and where you go in this life and the life to come.

Ask and it shall be given you, seek and you will find, knock and it shall be opened unto you. (Matthew 7:7)

Knocking and opening sounds like there are doors leading to your future and the things God has for you. So how do you know when to knock, and on what door? And when do you know when to keep knocking or to stop? Many people have different opinions on how to answer those questions. Jesus said:

Keep on asking, and you will receive what you ask for. Keep on seeking, and you will find. Keep on knocking and the door will be opened to you. (Matthew 7:7)

In another illustration, Jesus talks about prayer and knocking.

Then teaching them more about prayer, He used this story: Suppose you went to a friend's house at midnight wanting to borrow three loaves of bread. You say to him, A friend of mine has arrived for a visit, and I have nothing for him to eat. And suppose he calls out from his bedroom, don't bother me. The door is locked for the night, and my family and I are all in bed. I can't help you. But I tell you this-though he

> *won't do it for friendship's sake, if you keep knocking long enough, he will get up and give you whatever you need because of your shameless persistence.* (Luke 11:5-9)

It is an established fact from the Word of God that knocking and persistence for what we desire from God will result in His opening the door, provided that we ask according to His will.

> *And this is the confidence that we have in Him, that if we ask anything according to His will, He hears us.* (1 John 5:14)

Many people smile at the fact of God granting their request and opening a door when they ask, but they lose the smile when they are told that it only applies if they are asking and moving in the will of God.

Most people who lose the smile at the thought of having to be in God's will to receive an open door have never walked very far with Jesus. Those who have been down the road with Jesus for a few miles can look back and see God's hand of blessing by a door that stayed closed when they asked for it to be opened. They trust that if they follow the Word and persist and believe, doors will either open or stay closed to their benefit. They are never too timid to knock and keep knocking, but if the door stays closed, they move on in confidence as servants and not masters. If their Master wants the door opened, He will get it to open.

The Bible uses knocking and doors in many illustrations. The most important biblical illustration of knocking on doors is found in Revelation:

> *Behold, I stand at the door and knock, if anyone hear my voice and open the door, I will come in unto him and sup with him, and he with me.* (Revelation 3:20)

This illustration of knocking on doors is obviously more important than any other in the Bible. A person can have all of the world's best doors opened to them that allow for success and pleasures beyond imagination, and it would all mean nothing if the door of your heart was not opened when Jesus knocked.

> *What would it profit a man if he shall gain the whole world, and lose his own soul?* (Mark 8:36)

Anyone who prays to receive more of the Holy Spirit to enable them to reach the lost find a door that opens. And the more you are filled with the Holy Spirit, the more you will know what doors to knock on.

#39
Bobble Head

Most of us would like to know what the week will bring when we start out on a Monday. A lot of people would like to stretch that out to knowing what a month or a year will bring. If they knew what lay ahead, they could take advantage of the knowledge to make better decisions. Millions of people spend their time and money with astrology and fortune telling mediums trying to get a handle on what is coming their way but it is a waste of time to ask dead things (like cards and dice) and dead people (unsaved people going to hell) for what your future holds.

> *Someone may say to you, Let's ask the mediums and those who consult spirits of the dead. With their whisperings and mutterings, they will tell us what to do. But shouldn't people ask God for guidance? Should the living seek guidance from the dead?* (Isaiah 8:19)

God created everything:

Yours, O lord, is the greatness, the power, the glory, the victory and the majesty. Everything in the heavens and on earth is yours, O Lord, and this is your kingdom. We adore you as the one who is over all things. (1 Chronicles 29:11)

God controls how and when everything moves around you in sync with other things that are part of His plan. As you allow God to make you His answer to other people's prayers, He sends those who will be the answer to your prayers.

Jesus said that the most important commandment was:

Jesus replied You must love the Lord your God with all your heart, and with all your soul. And with all your mind. (Matthew 22:37)

If you love God the way Jesus said you must, then what is most important to God has to be important to you. Where you are going to be tomorrow, next month, or years from now should be centered on what is most important to the One who is most important to you.

There was a busy son who had an earthly dad who was a sold-out San Francisco Giants baseball fan. The dad wore only Giants t-shirts and hats. His car was plastered with Giants bumper stickers and he had a Giants bobble head player on the dash of his truck. This dad had Giants banners and flags flying in front of his house and all he wanted to talk about was what the Giants were doing.

Can this man's busy son claim that he loved his dad with all his heart and mind and soul if he never sat down to watch a Giants game on TV with his dad? Could this busy son say that his dad was the most important thing in his life if he never asked his dad to go to Pac Bell Park and watch a Giants game? Can he say that Dad is super important to him if every time Dad invites him to a game he says no?

Our Father in heaven is sold out on mankind. If God drives a truck in heaven it has a man and woman bobble head on the dash! God is the biggest fan of every human being on earth, and that is why His enemy works so hard to take what He loves the most away from Him.

If what you want to do, and where you want to go, is never about what God cares about most, then you are like the busy son who loves only in words without any actions to show that love.

If you love God the way Jesus says we must love Him, then the better part of our life will be spent looking for ways to bring to Him what is most precious to Him. If you love God, you can't just spend a few hours a month sitting in a pew without sharing His love with others. Your heart won't let you.

Those who love the Lord with all their heart, mind and soul will not all be doing the same things but the unified goal that everyone pursues will be the same, to bring what is most precious back to God. Each person will need the wisdom, help and guidance of the Holy Spirit to fit in where God has called them. Be confident that if your goal is to reach souls for Christ, God is right beside you because that's what He wants too. If you're not sure what to do, ask God for wisdom.

If you need wisdom, ask our generous God, and He will give it to you. He will not rebuke you for asking. But when you ask Him, be sure that your faith is in God alone. Do not waiver, for a person with divided loyalty is as unsettled as a wave of the sea that is blown and tossed by the wind. (James 1:5-6)

Once you realize the truth of what is being said, pursue it. Remember that we are all sold-out for Jesus and we are all on the same team. Don't be easily offended by others who can cause you to quit and lose out on God's blessings. Let your experience with caring about the lost deepen your relationship with God. When you talk with Him about the things He really cares about, you will enjoy His presence in a way you never have before.

#40
The Owr And Niyr

Thy Word is a lamp unto my feet and a light unto my path (Psalms 119:105)

Psalms 119 is the longest Psalm in the Bible and verse 105, has a message from God that can't be seen in the English language. The word used in the Hebrew for lamp is *Niyr*, which means *lamp, candle*. The word used in the Hebrew for light is *Owr*, which means *light of day, sun, stars, lightning*.

Most believe that King David wrote Psalms 119, but it doesn't really matter because all scripture is inspired by God and written for our benefit.

All Scripture is inspired by God and is useful to teach us what is true and make us realize what is wrong in our lives. It corrects us when we are wrong and teaches us to do what is right. (2 Timothy 3:16)

The psalmist knew more than anybody what it was like to receive a promise and then spend years trying to bring the promise into life.

The Psalm says that God's Word is an *Owr* in Hebrew—or *lightning* in English—to his path. If you have ever been in a thunderstorm at night where the moon is blacked out, all you can hear is the wind and you can see very little. When lightning flashes across the sky the darkness is obliterated, and you can see 50 or 100 miles in an instant. For a second or two you can see the outline of the horizon and hills, and then the darkness returns from where it went.

David said in Psalms 109, that the *Owr*, or flash of lightning, is when God showed him the path. In David's case, God sent the prophet Samuel to anoint him with oil to be the next king of Israel. That was the flash of the *Owr*, where David could see the far-reaching destination that God had for him from a shepherd boy to a king, and it was many miles and years ahead of him.

David experienced many trials and tribulations during his journey to be king. There were many twists and turns along the path as he made his way to his destiny that he saw in the moment of the *Owr*. The one thing David didn't see, and you won't see either, is a map on how to get there. Your faith in God and what He has shown you in the moment of the *Owr* is what will sustain you.

David says the Word is also a *Niyr* or a *candle* or *lamp* to his feet.

God's Word does both. He shows you the future with a flash of lightning and then leads you each day with a candle or lamp over your feet showing you how to get there.

When the Spirit of Truth comes, He will guide you into all truth. He will not speak on His own but will tell you what He has heard, He will tell you about the future. (John 16:13)

A candle or lamp does not give enough light to see in the dark for more than five or ten feet. A lamp will not show you where the road turns a half mile out or where a bridge is washed out in the canyon below. A lamp will only show you where to put the next step or two. This is by design. This is how God wants us to walk each day with faith in Him. When we reach a place where there is danger on the path, he wants us looking to Him for the answer. David lived his life this way, constantly consulting God along the path for solutions to the problems he faced. He kept going because of the *Owr* and the flash when God showed him his destination but he did it day by day and step by step with the light of the *Niyr* or the candle or lamp in his hand.

You may or may not have been anointed by a prophet, but God's Word says in many places what your future looks likes.

For I know the plans I have for you, says the Lord. They are plans for good and not for disaster, to give you a future and a hope. In those days if you look for me wholeheartedly you will find me. (Jeremiah 29:11-12)

And then He told them, go into all the world and preach the Good News to everyone (Mark 16:15)

The Lightning and the Lamp (the *Owr* and *Niyr*) is an important lesson to learn. Many people try and reverse the order and they never seem to get to far.

Exciting as it is to have the revelation and lightning flash before you, you can't walk each day by lightning. There are many people who travel to various and sundry places looking for a word and the lightning, but they have abandoned the lamp and the step-by-step process of reaching God's plan and His destiny for the life and future that He has already showed them.

#41
Two Down

What happened to the two groups of people who knew Jesus the best that caused them to doubt He was the Son of God and the promised Messiah? Both groups went down, and they were way, way closer to Jesus than anybody walking the planet today. If this is true, then how can anybody have faith and confidence that they won't go down too? The answer is simple. Find the common mistake that each of them made and then don't make the same mistake yourself.

The first guy that went down was John the Baptist and the disciples that followed him. When John ended up in prison for getting on the wrong side of Herod and it wasn't looking very good for him, John sent his disciples to talk to Jesus to see if he really was the Messiah. He wanted to know if there was someone else other than him that they were supposed to believe in and follow.

How could John the Baptist go down in flames as someone who would stop believing and having faith in Jesus as the Messiah? This was a guy who had no normal clothes or food or anything else that could be considered normal. He was sold out for God, living in the desert, a prophet that cared for nothing except preparing the way for the Messiah.

John was the half-cousin of Jesus. His mother, Elizabeth, was related to Jesus's mother Mary. John's birth was announced by the same angel, Gabriel, that announced the birth of Jesus six months later. John was filled with the Holy Spirit before he was even born, and he heard the audible voice of God confirming that Jesus was in fact God's Son.

But the angel said unto him, fear not, Zacharias; for your prayer is heard; and your wife Elizabeth shall bear you a son, and you shall call his name John. (Luke 1:13)

And it came to pass, that when Elizabeth heard the salutation of Mary, the babe (John) leaped in her womb and Elizabeth was filled with the Holy Spirit. (Luke 1:41)

And the same John had his raiment of camel's hair, and a leather belt about his loins; and his food was locusts and wild honey (Matthew 3:4)

But Jesus said, it should be done, for we must carry out all that God requires, So John agreed to baptize Him. After His baptism, as Jesus came up out of the water, the heavens were opened and he saw the Spirit of God descending like a dove and settling on him. And a voice from heaven said, This is my beloved Son, who brings me great joy. (Matthew 3:15-17)

> *Now when John had heard in prison the works of Christ, he sent two of his disciples and said unto Him, Are you He that should come, or do we look for another?* (Matthew 11:23)

With all that we know from the Word about John the Baptist, how could he go down, and if he did, what hope would we have to stand?

The second guys to go down were the disciples. They had spent three years traveling the road with Jesus and witnessing more miracles than could be printed in one book, and yet they all ran from Golgotha except John. If the disciples go down in unbelief that Jesus is the Messiah, what chance do we have to not go down too?

These super-anointed and knowledgeable people spent quality time with Jesus and were eyewitnesses to His power and miracles. If they ended up losing faith in their call, and the One who called them, what chance do you have that the same thing won't happen to you?

These two groups going down doesn't bode well for Joe Q. Christian until you see and understand why they went down. We have the benefit of looking back on the events in God's Word and learning from their mistakes. They fell off the ledge for a short time, but you don't have to.

Both groups made the same two mistakes:

1) Expectations
2) Circumstances

Their mistake was looking toward their own personal expectations and their surrounding circumstances.

If they were looking at what their scriptures said about the Messiah and what Jesus had said about Himself, they would have never had any doubt.

John didn't expect to die in prison, or he would not have sent his disciples to Jesus to look for another way or another Messiah. The *circumstances* that he found himself in were not what he *expected* and that is what caused him to lose faith in his mission. John had said,

He must increase and I must decrease, (John 3:30)

But he probably didn't expect that decreasing meant that he was going to prison to die.

The disciples had the same problem of expectations and circumstance. Even though they heard Jesus tell them on several occasions that he would be offered up as a sacrifice for many, and that he would come back from the grave, they thought He was speaking metaphorically or talking crazy. They didn't believe that it was actually going to happen. If they had taken Jesus at His word, they would have all been at the cross with John to support Him as He carried the sins of the world. If they had taken Jesus at His word, they would have all been gathered at the tomb with a cup of coffee waiting for Him to come out of the tomb instead of being huddled in a house hiding in fear.

Whatever God has called you to do, remember the two that went down and why. Don't make the same mistakes with expectations and circumstance. Leave the work you are called to do in God's hands and let things play out. Don't expect things to happen in a certain way, because it will almost certainly happen in a way you don't expect. Don't get rattled by the circumstance because they will be different than what you thought they'd be. Wait for things to develop and what might look like a loss or disaster can be the very thing God has planned to bless you. Unplug your clock and calendar. Don't let the timing of an event throw you off track. Keep your eyes focused on Jesus and you won't go down.

In a little while you will be with Jesus. Unlike the disciples not waiting at the tomb, Jesus will be waiting for you and He promises that your expectations and the circumstances of what is coming will blow your mind!

> *Eye has not seen, nor ear heard, and no mind has imagined what God has prepared for those who love Him* (1 Corinthians 2:9)

#42
3 P's

Everybody loves the last two P's and everybody hates the first P. Most people don't even want to talk about the first P and they run the other way if there is a possibility of the first P showing up at the party.

Others have manufactured arguments to convince you that the first P doesn't even exist. They will say that it's all in your mind or that the first P is just a reflection of your lack of faith and that you just need to believe there is no first P. They say there are only two P's for a real believer.

There are many more people who don't want anything to do with any of the P's, one, two or three. They want to slide by in life doing what they want to do, and they will accept nothing that may upset their apple cart.

Anyone who is called by God to further His kingdom will have to deal with the three P's. This is not an opinion but an obvious observation that anyone who reads the Bible can make.

Many people will not engage the enemy of God because of the fear of P number one.

The three P's are as follows and they almost always appear in this order:

1st P: Problems
2nd P: Provisions
3rd P. Promotion or Praise

Everybody loves to experience the supernatural provisions of God, or the second P, and no one hates the third P of promotion. As mentioned before, everybody would just as soon skip the first P. But you can't have the 2nd and 3rd P's without the first P.

Then call on me when you are in trouble, and I will rescue you, and you will bring me glory. (Psalms 50:15)

Can you see the three P's in what God is saying to you in this Psalm? They are different from the three P's above, but they are the same. The three P's in the Psalm are shown as three Parts:

1st P or Part is trouble: Problem
2nd P or Part is God rescuing: Provision
3rd P or Part is bringing Him Glory: Promotion

There is no glory to God without a rescue, and there can't be a rescue without a problem. Just as it's discussed above there is no third P without the first two P's.

There are dozens of stories in the Bible to illustrate and prove the point of the P's. We will use David because he was the one who wrote the Psalm with the three P's.

David was anointed to be king as a teenage shepherd boy. Not long after, he was presented with the first P or the Problem: Goliath.

Goliath walked out towards David with his shield bearer ahead of him, sneering in contempt at this ruddy-faced boy. Am I a dog he roared at David, that you come at me with a stick? And he cursed David by the names of his God's. Come over here, and I'll give your flesh to the birds and wild animals! Goliath yelled. (1 Samuel 17: 41-44)

Now that David had seen the first P up close, it was time to move to the second P or the Provision:

Today the Lord will conquer you, and I will kill you and cut off your head. And then I will give the dead bodies of your men to the birds and wild animals, and the whole world will know that there is a God in Israel. And everyone assembles here will know that the Lord rescues his people, but not with the sword and spear. This is the Lord's battle, and he will give you to us! As Goliath moved closer to attack, David quickly ran out to meet him. Reaching into his shepherd's bag and taking out a stone, he hurled it with his sling and hit the Philistine in the for head. The stone sank deep in, and Goliath stumbled and fell face down on the ground. (1 Samuel 17:46-49)

The second P or the provision came from God in the form of a proclamation of faith and the use of a stone. Then it was time to move to the third P, Promotion and Praise.

David defeated Goliath—he experienced the second P—and was given the third P of promotion into the king's family as the king's son-in-law.

The Bible say that God is an unchanging God. If His servants had to face obstacles or problems back then, you will have to face them now. The good news is that any problem you are facing now can be defeated by moving forward in faith in the Lord Jesus Christ. He will supply the second P if you'll trust Him and not be afraid. And you will shout the third P of Praise and Promotion!

If you are not facing any problem, that is when you should be afraid. That means you are not trying to do something that you can't do on your own, something you need help with. That means you are living a life without faith because you don't need faith to do what you can do without God's provision. And if you don't have that provision, that second P, there is not going to be a third P.

#43
Smorgasbord

Most of those who silence the ring tone and pocket their phone when God calls will never say that they shunned God's call. What they do is come up with excuses on why God doesn't want them to answer the call, and they actually end up convinced it's true. Most of them actually believe their own baloney and think God just dialed the wrong number.

The biggest and best weapon Satan uses to keep people from answering and being loyal to the call God has placed on their life is excuses. Satan doesn't have to convince most people to take an excuse from his Smorgasbord of tasty excuses. There are excuses of health, work, knowledge, time, family and many more. If one excuse doesn't fit quite right, they can grab another that fits better.

The deadly part about an excuse is that the one who uses the excuse begins to actually think they are justified by the reasons they give for not partaking in and supporting a ministry they were called to. You can't fix what you don't know is broken. If you think your excuse is justified and that God supports your decision, then there is no adjustment needed by you and your chance of being used by God is zero.

Most excusers feel that they are on a solid footing by not answering God's call, or not being loyal and dependable to ministry they said they'd support.

Two of Satan's favorite excuses that he puts up for grabs on his big Smorgasbord table of excuses are Family and Work.

Some Christians will say, *Oh I can't help with this or that because little Johnny has a soccer game that day. I know I committed to this or that but…*

They think it is more important to coach or watch Johnny than to be loyal to the work or ministry that God gave them, and they've been told by some idiot that it is okay. Using family as an excuse is the gold standard of excuses that Satan uses to keep people from experiencing the abundant blessings of following God and putting Him first in their lives, and everything else second.

Jesus is who we follow and not some fool who doesn't know what they are talking about when they say your family comes before serving Him.

> *If you want to be my disciple, you must hate everyone else by comparison to Me-your father and mother, wife and children, brothers and sisters-yes even your life. Otherwise, you cannot be my disciple* (Luke 14:26)

This verse found in Luke 14:26 doesn't mean you have to hate your family. It means you have to love them less than you love Jesus by comparison. What you love less gets less of your time, what you love more gets more of your time. The best excusers can't square that with their life when they tell you how much they love Jesus, so they learn to keep their mouth shut around people who are in the field of play.

What Jesus says are not His suggestions. He is not laying out multiple choices and allowing you to pick.

If you don't want to be a disciple or servant, fair enough, but at least make an informed decision that you are giving up the position as a disciple or servant by your actions. Don't believe the lie that says family matters and commitments give you a pass on putting what God has given you to do as a first priority in your life. Don't believe the false narrative that you can be unreliable and disloyal to God's call and still receive the same blessings as though you were a faithful disciple and servant. Most of the people who will tell you such lies have motives for not telling you the truth.

Serving God is not a hobby, you don't get to do it only when you feel like it, or if you have some free time on your hands. Serving God as a disciple or servant is a ministry and it takes priority over anything else, including work.

Some may say, "I can't spend money on the ministry because I have to save money to send my daughter to school." Why does somebody have to go to hell for your daughter to go to school?

If the funds that are needed for that ministry are put into your daughter's college fund, somebody is not going to be reached for Christ that otherwise would have. Why can't you be loyal to a ministry and trust God for your daughter's college education? Isn't God able to do both? The members of the excusers club serve as small god, not Jehovah God, because Jehovah God is able to do far above an exceedingly beyond anything we could hope for,

The second most favorite dish on the table at Satan's Smorgasbord of excuses is work. The excuses of work are usually used by inept Christians after they have used family as an excuse so many times, they have to change up the excuses to keep from being embarrassed.

If God can do anything, and if all blessings flow from heaven, why would you short God with your time and money using work as an excuse? If you put God first, what you do at work will be way more blessed than if you don't. There was a guy invited to the banquet in the Bible who said he had to work; it didn't go so well for him.

> *Another said, I have just bought five pairs of oxen, and I want to try them out, please excuse me.* (Luke 14:19)

This devotion #43 Smorgasbord is exciting, man!

This is an opportunity for someone to change up how they have been following God. If you want to be a disciple and servant of God and you haven't felt any direction or anointing, now you know why! Why would God give you the responsibility of a ministry as an answer to someone's prayer and then have you treat the ministry as a hobby? He would be letting down those who are counting on Him to come through.

Most people won't tell the truth about excuses because they don't want to make you feel bad, but that won't get you where you want to go as a disciple.

#44
Green Leaves

You have heard the saying that some look at a half a glass of water as half empty and some look at the glass as half full. People are all different and God loves every single one of them.

The ones who see the glass as half full are loved no more than those who see the glass as half empty. How we see things can make us more usable to further God's kingdom, but it doesn't make us more loveable to God. How we choose to look at things is really the difference in how we are used, not how we are loved.

If you choose to love God because you want to return the love He has given to you, then you must learn what He loves.

If you buy a jar of peanut butter as a gesture of affection for someone who is allergic to peanuts, the gift won't be accepted or eaten. If you offer a bottle Jack Daniels for someone who is thirsty and an alcoholic, what you're offering isn't a blessing – it's dangerous to them.

The Bible tells us what is pleasing to God, and what is not. If we want to return His love, we need to know what He loves so that we can offer it to Him. We know that God loves it when we have faith in Him and that we trust Him. We know that God takes no pleasure in doubt and unbelief in His abilities.

> *But without faith is impossible to please God: for he that comes to God must believe that He is, and that he is a rewarder of them that diligently seek Him* (Hebrews 11:6)

Every person on earth has an uncertain future. No one knows what tomorrow will bring. To some the uncertainty of the future is exciting as they trust God and move closer to the reality of Christ's return. They are looking forward to seeing Christ in the clouds and they trust God to bless them and use them as the days go by.

> *And then at last, the sign that the Son of Man is coming will appear in the heavens, and there will be deep morning among the people of the earth. And they will see the Son of Man coming on the clouds of heaven with power and great glory.* (Matthew 24:30)

Even as some anticipate the future with joy, others dread the future and try to plan a life that has more and more of everything on earth. For those, God becomes an unnecessary part of their lives and they can worship God at their leisure. When they offer their prayers to God from a place of unbelief in God's ability to provide for their future, their prayers are muted and go unanswered.

Those who dread the future and those who anticipate the future are both looking at the same thing. Neither knows what tomorrow brings. The future is controlled by God. Like those who look at a half a glass of water, both are looking at the same thing but see vast differences based on their faith in God. The one who trusts God is able to have a deeper relationship with Him because they pursue the life that is pleasing to Him. They trust God for good things tomorrow and that lets them offer Him good things today.

Those who don't trust God with their future are busy trying to fill the glass of the future with many things, so they won't have to depend on God. Their lack of faith shows in how they treat God and others with their tithes and offerings as they live a life that is pleasing to themselves rather than having a rich relationship with God. Jesus warned about those who try and build a future without pleasing God in Luke 12.

> *And He said to them, Take heed, and beware of the covetousness; for a man's life consists not in the abundance of things which he does possess. And He spoke a parable unto them saying, The ground of a certain rich man brought forth plentifully; And he said, This will I do; I will pull down my barns; and build greater barns, and then I'll have room enough to store all my wheat and other goods. And I'll sit back and say to myself, My Friend, you have enough stored away for years to come. Now take it easy! Eat, drink and be merry! But God said to him, You fool! You will die this very night. Then who will get everything you worked for? Yes a person is a fool to store up earthly wealth but not have a rich relationship with God.* (Luke 12:15-21)

God wants a rich relationship with every person on earth. It is hard to comprehend how someone so big and powerful can bend down to hear the smallest voice. Jesus referred to Himself as the Good Shepherd. I think there is something in the sheep and shepherd relationship that helps us to understand Jesus. He could have used any relationship on earth to describe the relationship between Him and us. And He chose the one of a shepherd and his sheep. He said that he'd leave his whole flock of 99 other sheep to come find the one who was lost and that says everything about how he feels about us.

> *If a man has a hundred sheep and one of them wanders away, what will he do? Won't he leave the ninety-nine others on the hills and go out and search for the one that is lost?* (Matthew 18:12)

A sheep loves to eat the green leaves off a tree in the field, but sheep are only able to reach up so high. When the shepherd comes and pulls leaves off the tree that is seven or eight feet up from the ground and higher than any sheep could ever reach, which sheep get the leaves from the shepherd's hand? The shepherd loves all the sheep the same but the ones who are near Him and pushing against his legs are the one who get the Green Leaves. He loves the sheep that are far off down the hill just as much as those pushing up against him, but those sheep are not close enough to get the Green Leaves.

The Green Leaves that the Shepherd offers us is the blessings of a rich relationship with Him.

#45
Port-O-Call

One day the Pharisees and Sadducees came to test Jesus, demanding that he show them a miraculous sign from heaven to prove his authority. (Matthew 16:1)

Watch out! Jesus warned them, Beware of the yeast of the Pharisees and Sadducees. At this they began to argue with each other because they hadn't brought any bread. Jesus knew what they were saying, so He said, You have so little faith! Why are you arguing with each other over having no bread? (Matthew 16:6-8)

There were two things going on with this ruckus on the boat. Jesus was saying *where is your faith to believe for food and why would you doubt that God can supply food after feeding of the multitudes*? And also, the priests were pushing doubt and false religion and He wanted them to pay attention.

When God performs a miraculous provision for you and then later when faced with the same circumstances and doubts, you can bet that the devil is trying to rob you of the faith you gained through the miraculous experience. The thoughts, or the yeast, that will start as a small thought in your mind will say, *Yeah God did this or that before. He paid the bill, kept me out of prison, healed my wife, but this time it's different. Your child is sicker than your wife was when God healed her.* Or the voice will say, *The debt is much greater than the debt God Miraculously provided funds for the last time and this time it's different etc. etc.*

This is how the yeast of hell is put into your mind to begin the expansion of fear and doubt. You can spot the age-old method that Satan uses to put this yeast into your mind as soon as you start to think and fear that maybe God can't come through this time. That somehow this time it's different. When you recognize that fear and doubt is trying to get a foothold in your mind, defend yourself! Use the Word of God to chop off the hand and fingers that are trying to put a pinch of the Pharisees yeast into your thoughts.

> *For God has not given us a spirit of fear and timidity, but of power, love and self-discipline* (2 Timothy 1:7)

> *We are human, but we don't wage war as humans do. We use God's mighty weapons, not worldly weapons, to knock down the strongholds of human reasoning and to destroy false arguments* (2 Corinthians 10:3-4)

> *Submit yourselves therefore to God, resist the devil and he will flee from you* (James 4:7)

Sometimes we think of resisting the devil as an exercise in looking the other way when we are tempted, and sometimes that's a good idea. In the case of resisting the yeast of the Pharisees and Sadducees the best way to resist is pro-actively. Start looking *at* something, not away from it. Start remembering what God has done in the past and know that there is no time or distance or limiting factors with God. He *will* do it again. The disciples had forgotten what Jesus had done before and that was one of the problems Jesus was putting His finger on when he said in the above verse (Mark 16:8) *You have such little faith.*

The second thing Jesus put his finger on as the yeast of the Pharisees and Sadducees was their teaching of false religion. Today there are billions of people condemned to hell for believing in false religions that started as a pinch of yeast from one dirt bag. A little twisting of a verse or two and entire religions are born that carry the curse of a pass to hell with them.

Let God's curse fall on anyone, including us or even an angel from heaven, who preaches a different kind of Good News than the one we preached to you. (Galatians 1:9)

The priests were denying the deity of Jesus and Jesus wanted them to pay attention. It wouldn't be long until Jesus would be gone, and then these guys would have to plow the road with what they were taught without Jesus physically being there. There were those who denied that Jesus was the Messiah then and there would be those who denied it later.

The Greek word in Matthew 16:6 above for *beware* is *Prosecho* which is defined as *be attentive, pay attention. as a ship coming port.*

When you're out in the middle of the bay or ocean, a few degrees off in the wheelhouse of your boat is no big deal. But when you are coming into port and docking the boat, the smallest error can be disastrous. Jesus was saying, *Hey man, you guys need to get this, you're coming into port and any mistakes you make are going to be magnified.*

The same admonition is given to us today. The time is short, and Jesus is coming back soon. We are coming into port and we have no room for false doctrines or playing church games. There is only one way to the Father and that is through the Son and now is no time to be entertaining a watered-down version of a politically correct religion.

Jesus is not *a* way to the Father; He is the one and *only* way to the Father. Keep this truth within you and there will be no yeast allowed to spoil what God is baking. Remember you are heading into port. Jesus is coming soon. Make every move count and pay attention

Jesus told him, I am the way, the truth and the life. No one can come to the Father except through me. (John 14:6)

#46
Left in Town

Nobody would say that they would put the life of a pigs before the life of a human being. The idea that a person would save the life of a pig over a human being would not be accepted in any society or culture. But what if the pigs were worth a lot of money and the human being wasn't worth anything because he was homeless, crazy and dirty? Most people would say that it doesn't matter how valuable the pigs are, they are not more valuable than a human being – until that human being started costing them money. They will wax philosophical with what you should do with your money, but things change when it's their money.

The pig farmers of Gerasene did not fear the man in the tombs with a thousand demons. How do we know? Because they went up and put chains on him again when he broke free. They didn't try to get rid of him or harm him, they left him up in the tombs howling.

Whenever he was put into chains and shackles-as he often was-he snapped the chains from his wrists and smashed the shackles, No one was string enough to subdue him. Day and night, he wandered among the burial caves and in the hills, howling and cutting himself with sharp stones. (Mark 5:4-5)

The people in the village were not afraid of the demon possessed man when he was running through the tombs naked and screaming, but now that he was fully clothed and sane, they were.

A crowd soon gathered around Jesus, and they saw the man who had been possessed by the legion of demons. He was sitting there fully clothed and perfectly sane, and they were all afraid (Mark 5:15)

To understand why they would be afraid now when they were not afraid before you have to go back to the previous verse.

There happened to be a large herd of pigs feeding on the hillside nearby. Send us into those pigs, the spirits begged, Let us enter them. So Jesus gave them permission. The evil spirits came out of the man and entered the pigs, and the entire herd of 2,000 pigs plunged down a steep hillside into the lake and drowned in the water. The herdsmen fled to the nearby town and the surrounding countryside, spreading the new as they ran. People rushed out to see what had happened. (Mark 5:11-14)

The people were not afraid of demons. They were not afraid of a crazy man stronger than anyone in town.

They were not afraid of raising food that was prohibited by the Jews to eat. But they were terrified of losing money. If Jesus had sent one farmer's huge herd of 2,000 pigs to their death, who would be next? They could all end up broke. This town had the Son of God at their disposal who could heal everyone from a crippled child to a blind grandfather. They could have heard about the plan of salvation from the architect of the eternity and spent forever in heaven. Great was the loss that they experienced that night, and they actually thought they were fortunate that Jesus left.

Money can obscure the things in life that are precious and get you to do things that you wouldn't think you would ever do. There were many people in that town that needed Jesus, just as there are many people in every town that need Jesus. And, because of money they didn't get a chance to see Him. The people pleaded with Jesus to leave and the man who was set free from the demons pleaded to go with Jesus.

And the crowd began pleading with Jesus to go away and leave them alone. As Jesus was getting in the boat, the man who had been demon possessed begged to go with Him. (Mark 5:17)

Jesus answered the prayer of the people who preferred the presence evil with money and denied the prayer of the man who preferred the presence of God. The people were willing to live with evil without being scared, but what really scared them was losing money. If they had embraced Jesus, they would have learned about increase without sorrow. They could have learned what true riches were and eternal life. They could have heard what Jesus had to say about eating pork and legitimized their business.

> *It's not what goes into your body that defiles you; you are defiled by what comes out from you heart.* (Mark 7:15)

Jesus sailed away that night with His disciples and left one man in town. This man was surrounded with people who cared nothing for the presence of God when it was compared to money and their business. The fact that they preferred evil made them evil themselves. Money will do that to people and the man left in town was going to be a daily reminder and a witness of the power of God and what His love could do.

> *And when He had come to the ship, he that had been possessed with the devil prayed Him that he might be with Him. Howbeit Jesus suffered him not, but said unto him, Go home to your friends, and tell them how great things the Lord hath done for you, and has had compassion on you. And he departed, and began to publish in Decapolis how great things had been done for him; and all men did marvel.* (Mark 5:18-20)

Many people today live and work in places where evil is preferred to righteousness. The citizens and employees allow evil to flourish in exchange for money. Small farming towns where God and family used to be important have been turned over to every evil practice under the sun. Big city towns turn the other way when the poor are ground up and their populations are decimated by the destruction of the unborn.

Just like Jesus did 2,000 years ago, He has left someone in town to show the great things that He has done for them. If you have been born again and you are surrounded by people where you live and work that prefer money to God, you are the one Jesus left in town. He left you in town, so you show people the great things God has done for you by your changed life.

Not everyone will want what God has for them still preferring evil and money over righteousness just like the farmers of Gerasene, but you were left in town to give God glory and honor for the things He has done.

#47
Front and Back Side

Most of us who have experienced something profound are different after the event than we were before the event. If we had a bad experience caused by the decisions that we made, we can purpose not to make the same decisions or mistakes again. Many times, when we try and tell someone our experience to help them, they don't listen, and they are doomed to make the same mistakes themselves. There is no substitute for first-hand knowledge and experience. That is what makes each of us who we are.

You shouldn't be too hard on yourself or others who have just come off the boat of a bad experience and are a little beat up. The journey they just took was designed to change them and it did! The tougher the journey, the more profound the changes that took place.

Unfortunately, we don't seem to change when multiple nice things are happening to us. When nothing but pleasant things happen, we tend to take some credit for them and get puffed up. That causes a change in the wrong direction.

2 Chronicles 34 and 35 tells the story of Josiah, a king who spent most of his life doing what God wanted him to do. He started as king when he was eight years old and reigned thirty-one years. Nothing but good things happened to Josiah most of his life as he led the people to remove the idols from the land. He restored worship of God and rebuilt the Temple of God. Josiah had one of the biggest Passover celebrations ever and his kingdom was at peace without any wars. There was nothing but good times for 31 years and then he went against God and was snuffed out because he never learned humility. Some may say that he had 31 good years and then died at 39, which isn't so bad, but that isn't the lesson to be learned. The lesson is that without times of trial and testing, our faith and character can't be built and some of the character traits that won't be gained will be needed later in our lives.

Humility can't be manufactured in a vacuum without the presence of some type of failure. Confidence can't be built after failure without a following success. God is responsible for both and He will give you both if you keep your eyes on Him.

The opposite guy in scripture from Josiah was Peter in the New Testament. He was prone to get himself in a bind by jumping into something, making an effort, and then failing. The famous story of Peter climbing out of the boat is one instance:

But Jesus spoke to them at once. Don't be afraid. He said. Take courage, I am here! Then Peter called to Him, Lord if it's really you, tell me to come to you, walking on the water.

Yes, come, Jesus said. So Peter went over the side of the boat and walked on the water towards Jesus. But when he saw the strong wind and the waves, he was terrified and began to sink, Save me, Lord! He shouted. (Mathew 14:27-30)

Peter wanted to be a man of faith who was successful in following what Jesus had for him to do. This is the same thing every believer wants but Peter kept falling short, like a lot of us do.

Peter thought he was saying the righteous thing and standing up for Jesus when he said, *Hey Man, this is not going down!* And then Jesus said he was speaking for Satan!

But Peter took Him aside and began to reprimand Him for saying such things. Heaven forbid, Lord, he said. This will never happen to you! Jesus turned to Peter and said, Get away from me, Satan! You are a dangerous trap to me. You are seeing things merely from a human point of view, not from God's (Matthew 16:22-23)

Peter thought he was right again when he talked about forgiveness. He also thought he was righteous when he told Jesus He couldn't wash his feet. And then he stumbled again and lied when he said he would never forsake Jesus. Peter had lots of failures, but they were preparing him for lots of successes.

Then Peter came to Him and asked, Lord, how often should I forgive someone who sins against me? Seven times? (Matthew 18:21)

When Jesus came to Simon Peter, Peter said to Him, Lord, are you going to wash my feet? Jesus replied, You don't

> *understand now what I am doing, but someday you will. No, Peter protested, you will never wash my feet! Jesus replied, Unless I wish you, you won't belong to me.* (John 13:6-8)

> *Peter declared, Even if everyone else deserts you, I will never desert you* (Matthew 26:33)

> *Peter swore, A curse on me if I'm lying-I don't know the man! And immediately the rooster crowed* (Matthew 26:74)

Peter had multiple lessons, some harder than others, but they all shaped who he would become on the back side of the cross. The failures occurred early when they didn't count so much on the front side of the cross before Jesus was crucified, and these failures shaped who he would become.

The trials you have gone through or that you may still be going through are designed for a purpose. You may not be able to know the purpose now, but God is using every disappointment and every tear to mold His servants into someone He can use. Peter couldn't understand why he kept screwing up, but each experience was specifically designed to enable him to succeed in the future. He was failing early when it didn't count so he wouldn't fail later when it did count.

Peter went from running away in fear from a little girl on the front side of the cross to standing up to Annas the High Priest and the council on the back side of the cross.

> *Later by the gate another servant girl noticed him and said to those standing around, This man was with Jesus of Nazareth.* (Matthew 26:71)

And now Lord, behold their threatening's; and grant unto thy servants, that with all boldness they may speak your Word. (Acts 4:29)

When Peter was praying to God for boldness, he refers to the priests and the council's warnings to keep quiet or else, as *threatening*. The word in the Greek is *Apeile,* which means *threatening, or a menace*. A menace is like a fly buzzing around your cheesecake. You just swat it away!

Peter had gone from the front side of the cross to the backside of the cross. His experiences and the power of the Holy Spirit changed who he was. The same Spirit that changed Peter is changing you. Don't beat yourself about the failures, it's a process.

The things that are threatening you are only a menace when you live on the back side of the cross. Satan will try and drag you around to the front side of the cross where there is no risen Savior who has been given all power and authority.

And Jesus came and spoke unto them, saying, All power is given unto me in heaven and in earth. (Matthew 28:18)

Satan has no power to return you to the front of the cross unless you give it to him. You will know that he is tugging on your shirt and trying to drag you to the front side of the cross when your problems are magnified in your mind to something more than just a menace.

Trust in a risen Savior on the back side of the cross. Use the Holy Spirit that resides in you to swat away the menace that is standing in the way of your victory!

#48
Shouting in the Temple

In the Bible we have an account of someone shouting in the temple:

> *Suddenly, a man in the synagogue who was possessed by an evil spirit began shouting. Why are you interfering with us, Jesus of Nazareth? Have you come to destroy us? I know who you are, the Holy One of God! Jesus cut him short and said Be quiet! Come out of the man, He ordered. At that the evil spirit screamed, threw the man into a convulsion, and then came out of him. Amazement gripped the audience, and they began to discuss what had happened.* (Mark 1:23-27)

When someone is teaching in the church and it is relatively quiet, someone who starts shouting is going to stop everything. The *shouting in the temple* stopped what Jesus was doing and changed, or took over, the agenda. What Jesus was saying was now being drowned out by what the demon was saying. The man and his demon had no right or authority to speak but the Word says *suddenly he shouted out* and by doing so he put himself in a position of authority. The man had a big mouth, and even though he had no authority or right to speak, he took over the position of authority by shouting over Jesus's words and disrupting the meeting.

The temple or synagogue today is your body that Christ and the Holy Spirit continually dwells in.

> *Don't you realize that your body is the Temple of the Holy Spirit, who lives in you and was given to you by God? You do not belong to yourself, for God bought you with a price, So you must honor God with your body* (1 Corinthians 6:19-20)

A Christian cannot be possessed by a demon, but they can be harassed and tempted by demons or the devil. The devil that came into the temple in Jerusalem to shout down the words of Jesus is the same devil that comes into your temple and he is still trying to shout down the words of Jesus.

You are the priest of the temple and you are the one who has the authority to dictate what takes place in the temple.

> *But you are not like that, for you are a chosen people. You are Royal Priests, a holy nation, God's very own possession. As a result, you can show others the goodness of God, for He called you out of the darkness into His wonderful light.* (1 Peter 2:9)

When you, as the priest of the temple, hear the voice of rg someone shouting and it is a voice that comes from the devil, you have the authority to silence him by exercising your God-given right by faith in Christ.

When God shows you what He has planned for you and the blessings He has in store for you there will always be some faith that is needed on your part to receive it. The Word says:

> *And it is impossible to please God without faith. Anyone who wants to come to Him must believe that God exists and that He rewards those who sincerely seek Him.* (Hebrews 11:6)

The devil will come into your temple and shout that what God says will not come to pass! He will shout that you can't rely on the Word of God! He will try and dissuade you from stepping out in faith to follow and believe what Jesus says. If the devil can get you to hesitate from moving in faith to receive what God has for you, he will mark that point of hesitation, and then he will furiously attack that place of hesitation with everything he has to breach the wall around your faith.

The first sign of a weakness in your faith is fear. The devil is always trying to find the place where there is fear hiding in the Temple so that he can try to exploit it. When God shows you the path to take, it will require faith on your part to step out. When the spirit of fear stands up and begins shouting in your temple, take the authority as the priest of the temple and command the voice to be silent and stand on the Word of God. There are many:

> *The Lord your God will bless you as He has promised. You will lend money to many nations but will never need to*

borrow. You will rule many nations, but they will not rule over you. (Deuteronomy 15:6)

He will tell you how you and everyone in your household can be saved (Acts 11:14)

Raise up a child in the way they should go and when they are old, they shall not depart from it. (Proverbs 22:6)

The thief cometh not but to steal, and to kill, and to destroy; I am come that they might have life, and that they might have it more abundantly. (John 10:10)

Who his own self bares our sins in His own body on the tree, that we, being dead to sins, should live unto righteousness: by whose stripes we are healed. (1 Peter 2:24)

You are the one who sets the agenda in the temple. Take authority and you be the one who shouts in the temple. Proclaim God's Word and attack the fear with the same force it attacked you with. Send that demonic voice packing to hell where it belongs. God made you the priest of the temple as part of a royal priesthood take your authority and clean house of any voices that exalt themselves above the Word of God.

#49
Bay See Lay O Hee Ra Tu Ma

#49 sounds like an ancient chant of some sort. It is ancient but it isn't no chant! The word this pronunciation refers to carries all the power and might of the universe for someone who'll take the title and run with it. It's a Greek word that is spelled *Basileious Hierateuma* and it stands for the English word *Royal Priesthood*.

> *But you are not like that, for you are a chosen people. You are a royal priesthood, a holy nation, God's very own possession. As a result, you can show others the goodness of God, for He called you out of darkness into His wonderful light.* (1 Peter 2:9)

If you are God's own possession, there is nothing that can harm you and nothing that you can't do in the quest to further the Gospel of Jesus Christ. You have access to the full weight and authority of heaven. When the things of this word have no hold on you, then there is no bait that you will chase to take your eyes off the things of heaven. The devil doesn't have any bait to use past this planet; he has no ownership of anything in the heaven where God resides. The only thing he has to offer after this life on earth is a hot seat.

If you are going to move as a royal priest, you're going to have to shed the desires for any of the bait the devil has in his bait bucket. God is not going to allow you to operate as *Bay-Se-Lay-O-He-Ra-Tu-Ma*, with His power and anointing, just to have you go chasing some guy or gal that jumped out of Satan's bait bucket.

> *Do not love this world or the things it offers you, for when you love the world, you do not have the love of the Father in you. For the world offers only a craving for physical pleasure, a craving for everything we see, and pride in our achievements and possessions. These are not from the Father, but are from this world.* (1 John 2:15-17)

> *Therefore, come out from among unbelievers, and separate yourselves from them, says the Lord. Don't touch their filthy things, I will welcome you.* (2 Corinthians 6:17)

Jesus said:

> *The world would love you as one of its own if you belonged to the world, but you are no longer part of the world. I chose you to come out of the world, so it hates you.* (John 15:19)

Jesus, John and Paul all said that we have to separate ourselves from the world. If you are ready to be *Bay-Se-Lay-O Hee-Ra-Tu-Mah* and push the kingdom there is a position waiting for you and it's not been assigned to you by a church Board of Directors. It is assigned to you by the Lord Jesus Christ Who sits at the right hand of the Father

If the world doesn't hate you, then you have not been pushing the kingdom of Jesus Christ. A kingdom today that doesn't accept multiple pathways to heaven and God is hated by the world. A kingdom today that doesn't tolerate every lifestyle's is hated by this world. A kingdom today that has walls and is not accepting of everyone who approaches it, is hated by the world.

As a royal priest you are not required to convince anybody that they should abandon their sin and ask Jesus to forgive them. You are only required to tell them that is required to enter the kingdom. What they do with the message is on them. You need the power of the Holy Spirit to succeed and when you lose affection for the things of this world you will have access to all the power you need.

In days gone by you may have needed a preacher or a prophet to reach the lost. Not anymore. Preachers can still preach and pray but now you can too as:

BAY-SE-LAY-O HEE-RAH-TU-MA!!

#50
Bear-Down

There are some problems that are more easily solved than others. If Jesus had to *bear-down* and move some things around sometimes to get things done, then so will you. You can't put God in a box and think that He will react the same way on every occasion. If He did, that would be a formula and you wouldn't need any faith. God is not a machine that you plug in that does the same thing all the time.

> *So you see, God chooses to show mercy to some, and He choose to harden the hearts of others so they refuse to listen* (Romans 9:18)

> *When a potter makes jars out of clay, doesn't he have the right to use the same lump of clay to make one jar for decoration and another to throw in the garbage?* (Romans 9:21)

In the story of Jairus and his sick daughter and the bleeding woman in Mark 5, there were many differences between the people involved who were touched by Jesus. What Jesus did with them was all different and not some kind of a formula.

- Jairus daughter was 12 years old.
- The woman who got healed from the issue of blood had been sick 12 years
- Jairus was a synagogue leader and the woman who was healed was banned from the synagogue.
- Jairus had an important position, the woman was penniless and unknown.
- Jairus sought Jesus out in the open as he got off the boat, the woman sneaked up in secret.
- Jairus wanted Jesus to touch his daughter, the woman wanted to touch Jesus.
- Jesus delayed healing Jairus's daughter and she died, He healed the woman on the spot.
- The woman got healed in a crowd, the daughter was raised from the dead with only a select few.

All of the crowd and commotion was moving together until Jesus heard that Jairus daughter was dead. From that point on Jesus started to *bear-down* to business. He encouraged Jairus to stay in faith and not run in fear and then he stopped the carnival of people from following Him any further.

> *While he was still speaking to her, messengers arrived from the home of Jairus, the leader of the synagogue. They told him, Your daughter is dead. There's use troubling the Teacher now. But Jesus overheard them and said to Jairus, Don't be afraid. Just have faith. Then Jesus stopped the*

crowd and wouldn't let anyone go with him except Peter, James and John. (Mark 5:35-36)

They must have been quite a distance from Jairus's house because if they were close by, they would not have sent messengers to save them the trip.

The time the disciples spent on the road from where the crowd was left behind and on the way to Jairus house was a silent sacred road where they had to *bear-down*, it was a time of pressing in and no distractions from the outside would be allowed, that's why the crowd was not permitted to go any further.

When you are headed for a difficult situation don't rush or cut the time short. Walk with Jesus and let Him strengthen you when the crowd is left behind, and you are alone with Him.

Peter, James and John had been together with Jesus twice before when they had to *bear-down* and there was no room for foolishness. Once on the mount of transfiguration and another time in the Garden of Gethsemane. All three times that Jesus separated the three from the crowd it was serious business.

Six days later Jesus took Peter and two brother, James and John, and led them up a high mountain to be alone. As the men watched, Jesus's appearance was transformed so that his face shined like the sun, and his clothes became as white as light. Suddenly, Moses and Elijah appeared and began talking with Jesus. (Matthew 17:1-3)

He took Peter, James and John with him, and he became deeply troubled and distressed. He told them, My soul is crushed with grief to the point of death, Stay here and keep watch with me. He went on a little further and fell to the

> *ground. He prayed that, if possible, that the awful hour awaiting him might pass him by.* (Mark 14:33-35)

Nobody knows exactly why Jesus chose Peter, James and John over the other disciples but it is clear that each time they were separated from the rest of the disciples when it was serious business and time to *bear-down*. Many say that they were separated for extra training because they were required to do more than the rest. It was probably because Jesus liked them. People tend to want their closest friends with them in serious times of need.

If you have ever been faced with a life and death situation it is comforting to have someone you care about and that cares about you present. Jesus wants to be that person who walks with you when it's time to *bear-down* and deal with tough issues. He understands what it means to be alone, He didn't want to be alone and He doesn't expect you to carry the burden alone either. He is right beside you if you ask Him to be, so next time you need to *bear-down* in a tough situation, get alone with Jesus for that walk up to the challenge you face, and remember Jesus knows what that's like. He is a friend who wants to walk with you away from the crowd. He said that He was.

> *Greater love hath no man than this, that a man lay down hi life for his friends. You are my friends, if you do what I command you to do. I no longer call you servants, because a master doesn't confide in his servants. Now you are my friends, since I have told you everything the Father told me.* (John 15:13-15)

#51
Wrong Again

If Jesus going to the cross was a fulfillment of Prophesy and spelled doom for Satan and his minions when He rose from the grave after the cross, then why would Satan scheme and lie to push Jesus to the cross? The answer to this question is simple, Satan misjudged the power of Jesus Christ, again.

Long before our world began, we have a record of Satan misjudging God's power

> *For you said to yourself, I will ascend to heaven and set my throne above God's stars. I will preside on the mountains of the God's far away in the north. I will climb to the highest heavens and be like the Most High* (Isaiah 14:13-14)

> *When the seventy-two disciples returned, they joyfully reported to Him, Lord, even the demons obey us when we use your name! Yes, He told them, I saw Satan fall from heaven like lightening!* (Luke 10:17-18)

Not even a fool starts a war they don't think that they can win, and Satan is no fool. Satan made a decision to go after God's throne based on what he saw. According to his calculations, he thought he could take God and he was confident enough to get some other angels to go along with him, but Satan miscalculated the power of God and was defeated.

Satan was observing Jesus the whole time Jesus was here on the earth. He knew that Jesus was the Messiah and tried to kill Him from birth. When that failed, he tried to derail him with pride in the desert, but Jesus was too strong for him. Then something changed. Jesus announced publicly that you no longer had to actually commit the physical act of sin, but you just had to think it in your heart, and it was sin

> *You have heard the commandment that says, You must not commit adultery. But I say, anyone who even looks at a woman with lust has already committed adultery with her in his heart.* (Matthew 5:27-28)

Satan knew Jesus was strong. They had fought against each before and Satan got the short end of that stick. Satan also knew how weak man was. He knew how weak men were in their body and in their minds, they were unable to resist his temptations. He had watched men give in to sin for thousands of years.

Jesus was fully man and fully God. Satan knew how strong the God side was and he knew how weak the man side was. Satan wasn't sure if Jesus on the man side of who He was could successfully live a life without sin. Nobody was able to do it before and you could bet that he was watching Jesus very closely from birth.

When Jesus said that a person could commit sin in his mind without the actual physical act, Satan figured he had Him. Satan knew there was no way that a man could go 33 years and never have an impure, angry or misplaced thought. Satan must have figured that Jesus went too far with that statement and overstepped the bounds of what was possible, so he kicked the plan in high gear and used evil men to crucify the Son of God.

When Jesus said *It is finished!*

Jesus knew His mission was now finished, and to fulfill Scripture he said, I am thirsty. A jar of sour wine was sitting there, so they soaked a sponge in it, put it on a hyssop branch, and held it to His lips. When Jesus tasted it, He said, It is finished! Then he bowed His head and release His spirit. (John 19:29-30)

There was nobody more surprised than Satan when the grave that had held down every other man in the history of the earth couldn't hold Jesus down. Satan was wrong again! He had misjudged the strength of the God-side of Jesus to enable the man-side of Jesus to blow apart his theory.

Because the grave couldn't hold Jesus for what a man thought or did, anyone else with faith in Jesus can't be held either. Jesus took the keys to death, hell and the grave and now we march forward to finish God's plan.

When we allow the God-side of who we are to strengthen the man-side of who we are, we will conquer Satan's plan against us every time

No weapon formed against you shall prosper, and every tongue which rises up against you in judgement you shall

condemn. This is the heritage of the servants of the Lord, and their righteousness is from Me, Says the Lord. (Isaiah 54:17)

The salvation that has been given you is like a diplomatic immunity pass at the airport that enables you to sail right through customs. You have diplomatic immunity from any wrongful acts committed while here on earth. You have heaven to represent while here on the earth, with a mandate to further God's kingdom and bring those who are lost in darkness to the light - so use the diplomatic immunity pass well.

Satan misjudged the power of Jesus and now he has no power or control over you. All he is left with is the ability to bluff. He will try and make you think that Jesus can't answer your prayers, but he is wrong again, because you know that He will!

#52
Reckless Faith

There is one Old Testament king you don't hear very much about. His name was King Jehu, and his story is found in 2 Kings 9. I think the reason you don't hear a lot about Jehu was that he was a wild man who had a Reckless Faith and that makes a lot of people nervous.

> *So a horseman went out to meet Jehu and said, The King wants to know if you are coming in peace. Jehu replied, What do you know about peace? Fall in behind me! The watchmen called out to the King, The messenger has met them, but he is not returning. So the King sent out a second horsemen, He rode up to them and said, The King wants to know if you come in peace. Again Jehu answered, What do you know about peace? Fall behind me!*
>
> *The watchmen exclaimed, The messenger has met them but he isn't returning either! It must be Jehu son of Nimshi, for he's driving like a madman.* (2 Kings 9:18-20)

The King James Bible says that Jehu rode furiously! The complete story of Jehu is in 2 Kings 9 and 10. Jehu was an officer in the military who was anointed by a servant of Elisha to be King and to clean house of some very evil people including the priests of Baal, Ahab and Jezebel. Jehu had some killing to do and some prophetic promises from God that needed fulfilling.

But Jehu drew his bow and shot Joram between the shoulders. The arrow pierced his heart, and he sank down dead in his chariot. Jehu said the Bidkar, his officer, throw him into the plot of land that belonged to Naboth and his sons that I saw yesterday. So throw him out on Naboth's property, just as the Lord said. When King Ahaziah of Judah saw what was happening, he fled along the road to Beth-haggan. Jehu rode after him, shouting, Shoot Him, too! So they shot Ahaziah in his chariot at the Ascent of Gur, near ibleam. He was able to go on as far as Megiddo, but he died there. (2 Kings 9:24-27)

The reason Jehu made people nervous back then is the same reason today. Jehu was a no baloney kind of guy who moved concisely and swiftly to get the job done that he was appointed to do. Jehu had a fearless and confident way about how he handled himself and he was no one to be trifled with. A man who moves quickly with power make people nervous. Just the same way that those around Peter got nervous when out of nowhere he jumps into the ocean when Jesus said to.

Most people like telling stories about guys that were bad back in the day, but then later they calmed down and became more statesmen-like. Jehu never did calm down. He was bad to the bone up to the end. One reason Jehu makes people nervous today is the fact that God used someone like him at all. Not only did God use him, but He instructed Elisha to anoint him king!

Jehu wasn't some poser king who stole the throne by assassinating somebody and stealing the throne. God made him king. If God did something like that back then, He could do something like that now, and there are some fire breathing servants of God who want to get with it for the kingdom of Jesus Christ.

God using some people like King Jehu now for ministry makes some nice people nervous. They don't want to think of these servants with Reckless Faith as being anointed of God and called for a purpose and ministry. If God used Jehu then, He could use these guys now!

If you take instructions from the Holy Spirit and jump when He is done speaking, then you probably make people nervous. Most folks who don't accomplish too much prefer a *let's have more meetings* approach to following God's instructions, and they talk a lot.

They will tell you that you need balance in your life, and they will tell you that your faith is reckless, and they don't mean that in a good way.

When you hear the comment or advice from others who say that you need *balance in your life*, ask them to explain King Jehu. Or ask them to explain how a teenager taking on a giant shows balance? You might ask them how a man who is 80 years old with nothing but a stick, who takes on the most powerful man in the world, is a balanced approach to life. While you're at it, ask them to explain a man named Gideon's balanced life when he agreed to fight 110,000 armed men with only 300 men that fought with horns and jars?

God has a job that needs to be done that not every servant can do. The men with Reckless Faith are prone to jump and go. They'd rather feel a hand on their chest telling them to slow down than a boot somewhere else telling them to speed up, they are a special breed who follow closely behind the Holy Spirit's lead.

Sometimes the mission calls for a man with Reckless Faith and those who don't have it don't understand it. But the men who have it are waiting for their opportunity to serve the King of Kings with everything they have and everything they'll ever have! Men with Reckless Faith believe what Paul said in Philippians 1:21

For me to live is Christ and to die is gain (Philippians 1:21)

If what you're attempting to accomplish for Christ seems impossible and crazy to others, maybe you were chosen for the task because of your Reckless Faith!

Index of Scripture References

Old Testament

Genesis 3:15 - #29 Straight Lines 108

Numbers 23:19 - #12 Following a Formula 32

Deuteronomy 15:6 - #48 Shouting in the Temple 191

1 Samuel 13:8-14 - #22 Robbed Patience 77

1 Samuel 16:7 - #26 The Chosen from the Called 94

1 Samuel 17:34-36 - #15 Sticks and Stones 45

1 Samuel 17:41-44 - #42 3 P's 165, #15 Sticks and Stones 45

1 Samuel 17:46-49 - #42 3 P's 165, #15 Sticks and Stones 45

1 Samuel 17:51 - #15 Sticks and Stones 45

1 Samuel 20:1 - #28 The Next Morning 103

1 Samuel 20:35-42 - #28 The Next Morning 103

1 Samuel 22:3 - #28 The Next Morning 103

1 Samuel 30:1-6 - #25 Winning and Losing 90

1 Samuel 30:17-20 - #25 Winning and Losing 90

2 Samuel 5:6 - #33 Lord of the Breaks 128

2 Samuel 5:17 - #33 Lord of the Breaks 128

2 Samuel 5:22 - #33 Lord of the Breaks 128

2 Samuel 11:1-2 - #2 Trouble is Born 3

2 Samuel 23:8,9 - #13 Fighters Fight 37

2 Samuel 24:24 - #6 Sacrifice 14

2 Kings 6:16-17 - #23 Enthused 81

2 Kings 9:18-20 - #52 Reckless Faith 206

2 Kings 9:24-27 - #52 Reckless Faith 206

2 Kings 13:18-19 - #23 Enthused 81

1 Chronicles 29:11 - #39 Bobble Head 152

2 Chronicles 34, 35 - #47 Front and Back Side 186

Psalms 2:4 - #29 Straight Lines 108

Psalms 50:15 - #42 3 P's 165

Psalms 51:11 - #7 Pride is Weak 16

Psalms 84:11 - #32 Storm's Coming 123

Psalms 119:105 - #40 The Owr And Niyr 156

Psalms 126:5-6 - #4 God Has Charts 8

Psalms 138:6 - #7 Pride is Weak 16

Psalms 145:1 - #28 The Next Morning 103

Proverbs 3:5-6 - #4 God Has Charts 8

Proverbs 11:14 - #27 Flip Side 99

Proverbs 22:6 - #48 Shouting in the Temple 191

Jeremiah 29:11-12 - #40 The Owr And Niyr 156 , #22 Robbed Patience 77

Isaiah 7:14 - #29 Straight Lines 108

Isaiah 8:8-10 - #29 Straight Lines 108

Isaiah 8:19 - #39 Bobble Head 152

Isaiah 11:1 - #29 Straight Lines 108

Index of Scripture References

Isaiah 14:13-14 - #51 Wrong Again 202

Isaiah 40:31 - #4 God Has Charts 8

Isaiah 54:17 - #13 Fighters Fight 37, #51 Wrong Again 202

Hosea 11:1 - #29 Straight Lines 108

Micah 5:2 - #29 Straight Lines 108

Habakkuk 2:3 - #32 Storm's Coming 123

Zechariah 1:9 - #5 Winnowing by the Winnower 11

Malachi 3:8-10 - #32 Storm's Coming 123

New Testament

Matthew 1:19 - #29 Straight Lines 108

Matthew 1:24 - #29 Straight Lines 108

Matthew 2:14 - #29 Straight Lines 108

Matthew 2:20-23 - #29 Straight Lines 108

Matthew 3:4 - #41 Two Down 160

Matthew 3:15-17 - #41 Two Down 160

Matthew 4:9 - #4 God Has Charts 8

Matthew 5:14-16 - #5 Winnowing by the Winnower 11, #8 Water That's Alive 19

Matthew 5:27-28 - #51 Wrong Again 202

Matthew 6:21 - #11 Great and Much and Many 29

Matthew 6:23 - #7 Pride is Weak 16, #11 Great and Much and Many 29

Matthew 6:24 - #11 Great and Much and Many 29

Matthew 7:24-27 - #34 Corners 132

Matthew 7:7 - #38 Doors 148

Matthew 8:22 - #36 Roof Wreckers 140

Matthew 9:38 - #16 Delayed for What? 49

Matthew 11:12 - #36 Roof Wreckers 140

Matthew 11:23 - #41 Two Down 160

Matthew 11:28-30 - #35 Come a Little Further 136, #11 Great and Much and Many 29

Matthew 12:30 - #13 Fighters Fight 37

Matthew 13:3-2 - #18 Four Seeds 57

Matthew 14:19 - #37 Half a Loaf 144

Matthew 14:29-30 - #1 Stepping Up and Stepping Out 1

Matthew 16:1 - #45 Port-O-Call 177

Matthew 16:6-8 - #45 Port-O-Call 177

Matthew 16:22-23 - #47 Front and Back Side 186

Matthew 17:1-3 - #50 Bear-Down 198

Matthew 18:12 - #44 Green Leaves 173

Matthew 18:21 - #47 Front and Back Side 186

Matthew 18:22-34 - #24 Talents and Pence 85

Index of Scripture References

Matthew 22:14 - #5 Winnowing by the Winnower 11 , #17 Faulty Filter 53, #26 The Chosen from the Called 94

Matthew 22:37 - #39 Bobble Head 152

Matthew 24:30 - #44 Green Leaves 173

Matthew 26:33 - #47 Front and Back Side 186

Matthew 26:71 - #47 Front and Back Side 186

Matthew 26:74 - #47 Front and Back Side 186

Matthew 28:18 - #47 Front and Back Side 186

Mark 1:1 - #34 Corners 132

Mark 1:23-27 - #48 Shouting in the Temple 191

Mark 2:1-5 - #36 Roof Wreckers 140

Mark 2:23 - #31 Walking Through 119

Mark 3:27 - #13 Fighters Fight 37

Mark 5:11-20 - #46 Left In Town 181

Mark 5:22-24 - #35 Come a Little Further 136

Mark 5:30 - #35 Come a Little Further 136

Mark 5:33 - #35 Come a Little Further 136

Mark 5:35-36 - #35 Come a Little Further 136, #50 Bear-Down 198

Mark 5:4-5 - #46 Left In Town 181.

Mark 6:45-47 - #21 What's the Problem? 73

Mark 7:15 - #46 Left In Town 181

Mark 8:36 - #8 Water That's Alive 19 , #11 Great and Much and Many 29 , #38 Doors 148

Mark 12:10 - #34 Corners 132

Mark 13:32 - #16 Delayed for What? 49

Mark 14:13-15 - #29 Straight Lines 108

Mark 14:27-30 - #47 Front and Back Side 186

Mark 14:33-35 - #50 Bear-Down 198

Mark 16:15 - #29 Straight Lines 108 , #40 The Owr And Niyr 156

Luke 1:13 - #41 Two Down 160

Luke 1:41 - #41 Two Down 160

Luke 3:17 - #5 Winnowing by the Winnower 11

Luke 7:14-15 - #30 One Day 114

Luke 7:7 - #30 One Day 114

Luke 8:25 - #30 One Day 114

Luke 8:26-39 - #30 One Day 114

Luke 8:45 - #30 One Day 114

Luke 8:5-15 - #18 Four Seeds 57

Luke 9:1-2 - #30 One Day 114

Luke 10:17-18 - #51 Wrong Again 202

Luke 11:13 - #19 No Man's Land 64

Luke 11:5-9 - #38 Doors 148

Luke 12:15-21 - #44 Green Leaves 173

Luke 12:48 - #8 Water That's Alive 19

Luke 14:19 - #43 Smorgasbord 169

Luke 14:26 - #43 Smorgasbord 169

Luke 14:28 - #27 Flip Side 99

Index of Scripture References

Luke 15:21-22 - #24 Talents and Pence 85

Luke 15:28-29 - #24 Talents and Pence 85

John 3:30 - #41 Two Down 160

John 3:5 - #8 Water That's Alive 19

John 4:10 - #8 Water That's Alive 19

John 6:35 - #35 Come a Little Further 136

John 6:37 - #35 Come a Little Further 136

John 6:5 - #8 Water That's Alive 19

John 6:63 - #8 Water That's Alive 19

John 8:7-9 - #2 Trouble is Born 3

John 9:4 - #3 Life is a River Not a Lake 6

John 10:10 - #48 Shouting in the Temple 191

John 11:14-15 - #9 Glad to be Dead? 23

John 11:5 - #10 Jesus Wept 26

John 12:6 - #20 What's In a Name? 68

John 13:30 - #20 What's In a Name? 68

John 13:6-8 - #47 Front and Back Side 186

John 14:6 - #45 Port-O-Call 177

John 15:13-15 - #10 Jesus Wept 26

John 15:13-15 - #50 Bear-Down 198

John 15:16 - #26 The Chosen from the Called 94

John 15:19 - #49 Bay See Lay O Hee Ra Tu Ma 195

John 16:13 - #40 The Owr And Niyr 156

John 19:29-30 - #51 Wrong Again 202

Acts 4:29 - #47 Front and Back Side 186

Acts 11:14 - #48 Shouting in the Temple 191

Acts 23:11-12 - #17 Faulty Filter 53

Acts 27:23 - #27 Flip Side 99

Romans 1:25 - #16 Delayed for What? 49

Romans 8:28 - #20 What's In a Name? 68

Romans 8:28 - #25 Winning and Losing 90

Romans 9:18 - #50 Bear-Down 198

Romans 9:21 - #50 Bear-Down 198

Romans 10:17 - #21 What's the Problem? 73

1 Corinthians 2:9 - #41 Two Down 160

1 Corinthians 6:19-20 - #48 Shouting in the Temple 191

1 Corinthians 10:13 - #4 God Has Charts 8

1 Corinthians 10:13 - #5 Winnowing by the Winnower 11

1 Corinthians 13:10 - #37 Half a Loaf 144

2 Corinthians 1:20 - #37 Half a Loaf 144

2 Corinthians 6:17 - #49 Bay See Lay O Hee Ra Tu Ma 195

2 Corinthians 9:11-12 - #16 Delayed for What? 49

Index of Scripture References

2 Corinthians 9:6 - #32 Storm's Coming 123

2 Corinthians 9:6-11 - #31 Walking Through 119

2 Corinthians 10:3-4 - #14 Yielding 41

2 Corinthians 10:3-4 - #45 Port-O-Call 177

Galatians 1:9 - #45 Port-O-Call 177

Galatians 3:5 - #4 God Has Charts 8

Galatians 5:1 - #19 No Man's Land 64

Galatians 5:4 - #19 No Man's Land 64

Galatians 6:7 - #31 Walking Through 119

Galatians 6:9 - #4 God Has Charts 8

Ephesians 1:4 - #26 The Chosen from the Called 94

Ephesians 2:8 - #7 Pride is Weak 16

Philippians 1:21 - #25 Winning and Losing 90

Philippians 1:21 - #52 Reckless Faith 206

Philippians 4:18 - #6 Sacrifice 14

2 Thessalonians 2:13 - #26 The Chosen from the Called 94

2 Timothy 1:7 - #45 Port-O-Call 177

2 Timothy 2:4 - #26 The Chosen from the Called 94

2 Timothy 3:16 - #33 Lord of the Breaks 128

2 Timothy 3:16 - #40 The Owr And Niyr 156

Hebrews 2:3 - #11 Great and Much and Many 29

Hebrews 4:15 - #14 Yielding 41

Hebrews 10:36 - #22 Robbed Patience 77

Hebrews 10:36 - #32 Storm's Coming 123

Hebrews 11:6 - #29 Straight Lines 108

Hebrews 11:6 - #44 Green Leaves 173

Hebrews 11:6 - #48 Shouting in the Temple 191

James 1:14-15 - #2 Trouble is Born 3

James 1:5-6 - #39 Bobble Head 152

James 4:14 - #3 Life is a River Not a Lake 6

James 4:17 - #14 Yielding 41

James 4:6 - #26 The Chosen from the Called 94

James 4:7 - #45 Port-O-Call 177

1 Peter 1:7 - #5 Winnowing by the Winnower 11

1 Peter 2:24 - #48 Shouting in the Temple 191

1 Peter 2:9 - #48 Shouting in the Temple 191

1 Peter 2:9 - #49 Bay See Lay O Hee Ra Tu Ma 195

2 Peter 3:9 - #16 Delayed for What? 49

1 John 2:15-17 - #49 Bay See Lay O Hee Ra Tu Ma 195

1 John 3:22 - #32 Storm's Coming 123

1 John 4:4 - #13 Fighters Fight 37

Index of Scripture References

1 John 5:14 - #38 Doors 148

1 John 5:15 - #16 Delayed for What? 49

Revelation 3:20 - #38 Doors 148

Scripture by Devotional

#1 Stepping Up and Stepping Out, Page 1
   Matthew 14:29-30

#2 Trouble is Born, Page 3
   2 Samuel 11:1-2
   John 8:7-9
   James 1:14-15

#3 Life is a River Not a Lake, Page 6
   John 9:4
   James 4:14

#4 God Has Charts, Page 8
   Psalms 126:5-6
   Proverbs 3:5-6
   Isaiah 40:31
   Matthew 4:9
   Galatians 3:5, 6:9
   1 Corinthians 10:13

#5 Winnowing by the Winnower, Page 11
   Zechariah 1:9
   Matthew 5:14-16, 22:14
   Luke 3:17
   1 Corinthians 10:13
   1 Peter 1:7

#6 Sacrifice, Page 14
   2 Samuel 24:24
   Philippians 4:18

#7 Pride is Weak, Page 16
   Psalms 51:11 , 138:6
   Matthew 6:23
   Ephesians 2:8

#8 Water That's Alive, Page 19
   Matthew 5:14-16
   Mark 8:36
   Luke 12:48
   John 3:5, 4:10, 6:5, 6:35, 6:63

#9 Glad to be Dead? , Page 23
   John 11:14-15

#10 Jesus Wept, Page 26
   John 11:5, 15:13-15

#11 Great and Much and Many, Page 29
   Matthew 6:21, 6:23, 6:24, 11:30
   Mark 8:36
   Hebrews 2:3

#12 Following a Formula, Page 32
   Numbers 23:19

#13 Fighters Fight, Page 37
   2 Samuel 23:8,9
   Isaiah 54:17
   Matthew 12:30
   Mark 3:27
   1 John 4:4

#14 Yielding, Page 41
   2 Corinthians 10:3-4
   Hebrews 4:15
   James 4:17

#15 Sticks and Stones, Page 45
   1 Samuel 17:34-36, 17:41-44, 17:46-49, 17:51

#16 Delayed for What? , Page 49
   Matthew 9:38
   Mark 13:32
   Romans 1:25
   2 Corinthians 9:11-12
   2 Peter 3:9
   1 John 5:15

#17 Faulty Filter, Page 53
   Matthew 22:14
   Acts 23:11-12

#18 Four Seeds, Page 57
   Matthew 13:3-2
   Luke 8:5-15

#19 No Man's Land, Page 64
   Luke 11:13
   Galatians 5:1, 5:4

#20 What's In a Name? , Page 68
   John 12:6, 13:30
   Romans 8:28

#21 What's the Problem? , Page 73
   Romans 10:17
   Mark 6:45-47

Scripture by Devotional

#22 Robbed Patience, Page 77
  1 Samuel 13:8-14
  Jeremiah 29:11-12
  Hebrews 10:36

#23 Enthused, Page 81
  2 Kings 6:16-17 , 13:18-19

#24 Talents and Pence, Page 85
  Matthew 18:22-34
  Luke 15:21-22, 15:28-29

#25 Winning and Losing, Page 90
  1 Samuel 30:1-6 , 30:17-20
  Romans 8:28
  Philippians 1:21

#26 The Chosen from the Called, Page 94
  1 Samuel 16:7
  Matthew 22:14
  John 15:16
  2 Thessalonians 2:13
  2 Timothy 2:4
  Ephesians 1:4
  James 4:6

#27 Flip Side, Page 99
  Proverbs 11:14
  Luke 14:28
  Acts 27:23

#28 The Next Morning, Page 103
  1 Samuel 20:1, 20:35-42, 1 Samuel 22:3
  Psalms 145:1

#29 Straight Lines, Page 108
  Genesis 3:15
  Psalms 2:4
  Isaiah 7:14, 8:8-10, 11:1
  Hosea 11:1
  Micah 5:2
  Matthew 1:19, 1:24, 2:14, 2:20-23
  Mark 14:13-15, 16:15
  Hebrews 11:6

#30 One Day, Page 114
  Luke 7:7, 7:14-15, 8:25-39, 8:45, 9:1-2

#31 Walking Through, Page 119
  Mark 2:23
  Galatians 6:7
  2 Corinthians 9:6-11

#32 Storm's Coming, Page 123
  Malachi 3:8-10
  Psalms 84:11
  Habakkuk 2:3
  2 Corinthians 9:6
  Hebrews 10:36
  1 John 3:22

#33 Lord of the Break, Page s 128
  2 Samuel 5:6, 5:17, 5:22
  2 Timothy 3:16

#34 Corners, Page 132
  Matthew 7:24-27
  Mark 1:1, 12:10

#35 Come a Little Further, Page 136
  Mark 5:22-24, 5:30, 5:33, 5:35-36
  John 6:37
  Matthew 11:28-30

#36 Roof Wreckers, Page 140
  Matthew 8:22, 11:12
  Mark 2:1-5

#37 Half a Loaf, Page 144
  Matthew 14:19
  1 Corinthians 13:10
  2 Corinthians 1:20

#38 Doors, Page 148
  Matthew 7:7
  Mark 8:36
  Luke 11:5-9
  1 John 5:14
  Revelation 3:20

#39 Bobble Head, Page 152
  Matthew 22:37
  James 1:5-6
  1 Chronicles 29:11
  Isaiah 8:19

#40 The Owr And Niyr, Page 156
  Psalms 119:105
  Jeremiah 29:11-12
  Mark 16:15

Scripture by Devotional

John 16:13
2 Timothy 3:16

#41 Two Down, Page 160
Matthew 3:4, 3:15-17, 11:23
Luke 1:13, 1:41
John 3:30
1 Corinthians 2:9

#42 3 P's, Page 165
1 Samuel 17:41-44, 17:46-49
Psalms 50:15

#43 Smorgasbord, Page 169
Luke 14:19 14:26

#44 Green Leaves, Page 173
Matthew 18:12, 24:30
Luke 12:15-21
Hebrews 11:6

#45 Port-O-Call, Page 177
Matthew 16:1, 16:6-8
2 Corinthians 10:3-4
Galatians 1:9
2 Timothy 1:7
James 4:7

#46 Left In Town, Page 181
Mark 5:4-5, 5:11-20, 7:15

#47 Front and Back Side, Page 186
2 Chronicles 34, 35
Matthew 16:22-23, 18:21, 26:33, 26:71, 26:74, 28:18
Mark 14:27-30
John 13:6-8
Acts 4:29

#48 Shouting in the Temple, Page 191
Deuteronomy 15:6
Proverbs 22:6
Mark 1:23-27
John 10:10
Acts 11:14
1 Corinthians 6:19-20
Hebrews 11:6
1 Peter 2:9, 2:24

#49 Bay See Lay O Hee Ra Tu Ma, Page 195
John 15:19
2 Corinthians 6:17
1 Peter 2:9
1 John 2:15-17

#50 Bear-Down, Page 198
Matthew 17:1-3
Mark 5:35-36, 14:33-35
John 15:13-15
Romans 9:18, 9:21

#51 Wrong Again, Page 202
Isaiah 14:13-14, 54:17
Matthew 5:27-28
Luke 10:17-18
John 19:29-30

#52 Reckless Faith, Page 206
2 Kings 9:18-20, 9:24-27
Philippians 1:21

About Ben Hardister

Ben Hardister is the President of the Soldiers Of The Cross Motorcycle Ministry (SOTC) in Modesto, CA Ben with the members of SOTC have shown what a small group of 70 men can accomplish to advance the Kingdom of God in the world when they decide to walk by faith and not by sight. This book of 52 Devotions follows Ben's first book "Faith without honor and dogs that can't hunt" and each devotion is taken from the Gospel teaching Ben has shared each week at the SOTC weekly Bible study. In the past five years Ben and the men who are SOTC have donated over One Million Dollars for numerous missions and facilities to honor God and reach the lost in Sighisoara Romania, Phnom Penh, Cambodia, Battambong, Cambodia, Tecate, Mexico, and many other cities throughout California including the Central Valley and San Francisco. Ben continues to develop agricultural land and farming for income while putting into practice the truths of the Scripture that says when we move God moves and He continues to help teach men these same principals and encourage them to have a rich relationship towards God.

Made in the USA
Columbia, SC
17 June 2024